Ideas and Structures

Ideas and Structures

Essays in Architectural History

ALMANTAS SAMALAVIČIUS

RESOURCE *Publications* • Eugene, Oregon

IDEAS AND STRUCTURES
Essays in Architectural History

Copyright © 2011 Almantas Samalavičius. All rights reserved. Except for brief quotations in critical publications or reviews, no part of this book may be reproduced in any manner without prior written permission from the publisher. Write: Permissions, Wipf and Stock Publishers, 199 W. 8th Ave., Suite 3, Eugene, OR 97401.

Resource Publications
An Imprint of Wipf and Stock Publishers
199 W. 8th Ave., Suite 3
Eugene, OR 97401

www.wipfandstock.com

ISBN 13: 978-1-60899-736-7

Manufactured in the U.S.A.

Contents

Preface   vii

Acknowledgments   xi

1   Architecture and Light   1

2   Architecture and Color   28

3   Architecture and Sound   58

4   Architecture and Water   85

Bibliography   111

Preface

THIS BOOK IS A scholarly inquiry into several aspects of architecture viewed from the perspective of the history of ideas. It is a text of interdisciplinary character, involving interpretations and documentation drawn from philosophy, history, and architectural theory, as well as religious studies and symbology. By combining these different perspectives, the aim is to present an overview of the development of ideas and forms in architecture—that is, light, color, sound, and water, and the shifts in their relationship to architecture from ancient times to the modern era.

The first chapter, "Architecture and Light," starts with an exploration of concepts emphasizing the divinity of light that flourished in most ancient civilizations (Egyptian, Greek, Roman, etc.). Examples show how deeply the understanding of light was linked to divine powers in archaic mythology and other sources of ancient thinking. The continuation of this tradition is traced from Pythagoras to Plato and the Neoplatonists, and then to the medieval philosophy of St. Augustine. The dualism of the conception of light in medieval Christian philosophy and theology—between light and its divine source—is emphasized by overviewing the ideas expressed by such thinkers as Johannes Scotus Eriugena, Hugh of St. Victor, St. Bonaventure, and others who continued the tradition established by Pseudo-Dionysius (or Dionysius the Areopagite), who claimed that all of God's creation is a light that illuminates the mind. The attempt of Abbot Suger, the builder and author of the iconographical program of St. Denis Cathedral, to glorify divine light is outlined as a basis for discussion of the illumination of Gothic cathedrals and the employment of stained glass in Western religious architecture. Ideas about the divine character of light persisted even after the waning of the Middle Ages, as can be seen through the writings of the Christian mystics. Renaissance thinkers such as Marsilio Ficino are briefly discussed in relation to their revival of the solar cult. On the other hand, doctrines developed by such mystics as Jacob Boehme and the alchemists Robert Fludd and Johannes Kepler have also contributed to the subject matter. The peculiarities of interior lightning in Baroque churches are brought into consideration with explicit examples ranging from Italian to Lithuanian Baroque structures. The chapter continues with an overview of new philosophical thinking about architecture during the Enlightenment and the application of light into building structures.

Principles of lighting in the architecture of modern times has been treated by such important architects as Frank Lloyd Wright, Le Corbusier, and later Louis I. Kahn. It is obvious that a true understanding of the role and importance of natural light is yet evolving, given the controversies regarding technological progress, but the phenomenon of light still bears a metaphysical dimension.

The second chapter, "Architecture and Color," is a historical reconsideration of the role of color in architecture. The first attempts by ancient civilizations to theoretically comprehend the nature of color are discussed. The weakness of the treatment of color in the writings of Plato is exposed, and contrasted with explanations offered by Aristotle and Plotinus. The essay proceeds to a discussion of Vitruvius, the first known western theorist of architecture, who wrote extensively about color in architecture and its technological applications. The medieval understanding of color is analyzed, drawing on examples from Thomas Aquinas and other Christian thinkers of the period. Because the mixing of elements was directly linked to the deeds of Satan, the use of pure colors prevailed throughout almost all the Middle Ages. The relationship of color and light in medieval architecture is emphasized. New concepts of color that emerged during the Enlightenment are explored: the influence of research by Issac Newton and other early scientists is evaluated, and their impact on later scholars like Johann Wolfgang Goethe, who rejected some of Newton's ideas, are discussed.

The chapter provides an interpretation of the concepts of color worked out by highly innovative modern artists of the twentieth century, such as Wassily Kandinsky and Fernand Leger. The symbolism of color is treated in a separate section, where the approaches offered by various scholars, ranging from metaphysics to positivism, are summarized. The last section traces the evolution of color schemes in western urban areas and its dependency on local materials, traditions, and building practices.

The colors used in architectural decoration in the ancient civilizations of Egypt, Greece, China, and India are briefly discussed. The color schemes of medieval, Renaissance, and baroque architectural buildings are shown to represent the different attitudes towards decoration that dominated in these epochs. Attempts to relate architectural colors schemes to "national character" during the rise of the national states are reviewed. The color schemes preferred by leading modern architects are brought into scrutiny, and the chapter concludes with remarks on the grayness and dullness of communist/Soviet architecture and the "wild" use of colors in post-communist Eastern Europe.

The third chapter, "Architecture and Sound," covers a somewhat more esoteric subject—the relationship between the musical harmony theory invented by Pythagoras and his disciples and the architecture of various periods of history. The persistence of analogies between principles of music and architecture is outlined by bringing together the most essential examples from different epochs and cultures. The first section reconsiders the birth of musical theory, which originated in Greece with the Orphic religion and was continued by Pythagoras and his school, the first to prove rationally that there exists a relationship between musical intervals and proportions. Theories on the connection between musical and architectural proportions and their dependence on numbers continued developing. The later writings of Plato indicate that he had finally adopted a Pythagorean approach. Later authors, like the Roman architectural theorist Vitruvius, passed on the tradition to the Middle Ages. St. Augustine, Boethius, and Hugh of St. Victor continued to develop ideas of harmony, and were preoccupied with studies of the structure of music. Philosophical metaphors of God as an elegant architect who turned the universe into his palace had a direct influence on architectural practice. Structures were erected according to proportions that were derived from music and numbers. The architecture of Renaissance represents a true rebirth of the Pythagorean spirit: most architects applied principles of music to their buildings, including Andrea Palladio, Leon Battista Alberti, and other distinguished architects. The analogy between sound and the cosmos was developed further in the Baroque period by such authors as Fludd, Kircher, and Kepler. Ideas of this kind lost their relevance with the advance of the Enlightenment, but were eventually revived in the nineteenth century, due to the work of the eccentric scholar Albert von Thimmus. The last section is a very brief historical overview of architectural acoustics, demonstrating the differences between medieval churches, where sound and chant were closely related, and the architecture of later periods, when, paradoxically, the rise of technological progress in a way ended the "culture of hearing" in architecture, and turned architectural structures into "mute" and "deaf" buildings.

The fourth chapter, "Architecture and Water," traces the development of technologies related to water usage in urban cultures and changes in the metaphysical concepts of water as a substance. Its first section is a discussion of the understanding of water as a primal substance and one of the elements informing the structure of Nature. The writings of Vitruvius illustrate the depth of Roman knowledge about water and water supplies. Numerous technologies for water supply were invented by the Romans, whose "culture of water" was highly developed for recreational, hygienic, and other purposes. The most outstanding examples of Roman baths and villas, their peculiarities, and their impact upon water culture in later periods of history are discussed. A separate section is dedicated to the explanation of water symbolism in Christian faith and rituals. Drawing on medieval sources of Christian symbology, an overview of the meaning and forms of baptizing and the baptisteries in which the rituals were performed is included. An interpretation of water symbolism in the process of erecting edifices has been among those aspects that interested me in this book.

The practical usage of water and the technologies that provided it to towns and cities in medieval times is briefly discussed in the following section. Special attention is given to the much more important aesthetic and recreational role of water during the Renaissance, when Italian nobility and clergy built numerous breath-taking suburban residences in picturesque natural surroundings, as well as to the continuation of this tradition in the Baroque era. The advent of modern times was marked by striving for lighter and more hygienic urban spaces. The rise of the mechanistic concept of treated water as a technological means for washing away human waste is a topic briefly touched on, but obviously needs more reflection. Meanwhile I have attempted to show that despite the degradation of water to the level of a mere industrial substance, the need for a philosophical and aesthetic understanding of water in contemporary architecture continues to exist.

Acknowledgments

I WOULD LIKE TO extend warm thanks to several colleagues who helped to shape this book during different stages of writing. I would particularly like to thank Professor Rimantas Buivydas, Dean of the Architectural Faculty of my home university, who a decade ago skillfully guided me into these issues and then kindly encouraged me to contribute several articles to *Archiforma/Lithuanian Architectural Review*—a journal which he founded and edited during that early period when my interest in the history of architectural ideas matured. My thanks also go to professors Carmen Ferrando and Javier Celicelanea of Basque University's School of Architecture in San Sebastian, who kindly invited me to give a graduate seminar on one of the themes explored in this book, as well as Professor Jaime Navarro Casas, who provided an opportunity to lecture to a dedicated group of scholars at his School of Architecture at the University of Seville, and Professor Lech Sokol of Warsaw School of Social Psychology, who kindly invited me to talk on light and architecture at his international seminar. I am also very grateful to Dr. Andrzej Ekwinski, director of the Vardo-Seminar Foundation, Stockholm, who appeared *ex nihilo* and provided me with a wonderful intellectual milieu in which to develop an interdisciplinary approach towards art and architecture while attending his memorable seminars in Sweden, Finland, and Poland for nearly two decades. My students at Vilnius Gediminas Technical University, Faculty of Architecture, who attended my graduate seminars on architectural aesthetics and architectural criticism, were a rewarding audience to further encourage me to pursue this on-going investigation into the history of architectural ideas. I would like to thank my editor Elisabeth Novickas for her invaluable help.

1

Architecture and Light

In the penetrating short story "Alef," Jorge Louis Borges describes a mystical source of light that opens under a staircase in a cellar somewhere on the outskirts of Buenos Aires. A tiny globe that can be taken into the cup of one's hand shines in the colors of a sunflower, and the protagonist of this striking story is deprived of speech by the transparency and brightness of the globe's rays. It is a point where all the points of the universe meet, and while focusing one's eyes on Alef one can see all the possible angles of this world, which miraculously open themselves to visual perception. By exposing the metaphysical aspects of being, Borges brings his readers to a dimension that is not so much associated with the power of human sight as it is with the powers of the soul to comprehend the incomprehensible, to perceive what is imperceptible to the naked eye. In describing this mystical vision, Borges approaches a tradition of metaphysical thinking that is thousands of years old, when the inner sight, inspired by illuminating light, was treated as a manifestation of divine will and grace. In old metaphysical doctrines, light was interpreted as a symbol of morality, reason, and the seven virtues: to be illuminated meant gaining an understanding about the existence of the source of light, and this provided spiritual power to a human being.[1]

THE DIVINITY OF LIGHT IN ANCIENT CIVILIZATIONS

It is obvious that light is an essential condition of human and planetary existence: as it is directly related to warmth, it predetermines the survival

---

1. Cirlot, *Dictionary of Symbols*, 187–88.

of human beings in the world. No wonder then, that man's attempts to comprehend and explain the origin of this mysterious phenomenon date to ancient times. In the mythic consciousness, light was related to divinity. Evidence of this primeval concept is found in the vocabularies of many ancient cultures: the word stem *div-* or *dyu-*, found in the Aryan language, meant "to shine"; the notion *deva* (god) originated from the former, while *Dyaus* and his brothers Zeus and Jupiter from the latter. In Sanskrit—the parent language of Indo-European—the noun *dyu* means two things: the sky and the day. Furthermore, the Greek prayer "Rain, rain, dear Zeus, on Athenian lands and fields," mentioned by Marcus Aurelius, Homer, and Petronius, sheds light on the origin of Zeus' name: from the very beginning the bright sky was called by this name; gradually the Greeks and later the Romans forgot the earlier meaning of the word.[2] Macrobius, whose authority on spiritual matters was greatly valued and considered indisputable during the Middle Ages, claimed that these lines of Orpheus are direct reflections on the light-providing omnipotence of the sun: "Hear, o Thou who dost, wheeling afar, ever make the turning circle of rays to revolve in its heavenly orbits, bright Zeus Dionysus, Father of Sea, Father of Land, source of all Life, all-gleaming with thy golden light."[3]

Archaic myths, although the meaning of their content changed as time went by, are full of stories relating how light defeats the darkness and makes its appearance in the world. In the well-known myth of the ancient world about Oedipus, the Theban hero is a personification of sunrise and sunset. After the Delphic Oracle predicts that when the boy grows up he will kill his father and marry his mother, the new-born baby is left in the forest at the order of his father; however, while left alone in the heart of dark woods, the child is saved by passers-by. When the boy grows up, he returns to his birth-place, and quarrels and then kills an old man he meets on the road; eventually he rescues the town from the Sphinx and gets the whole kingdom and a bride as a reward. His bride, however, perishes as soon as she discovers the truth, while Oedipus pokes out his eyes and dies. The anthropomorphic and moral meaning of incest was extracted from the myth by the Greeks somewhat later; in the very beginning this was a story relating how the sun rises, defeating the Vedic demon of darkness, and is united in the evening with the dawn that gave birth to him. It is suggested that the etymology of the names of

2. Fiske, *Myths and Myth-Makers*, 286.
3. Macrobius, *Saturnalia*, 153.

the heroes implies the original meaning of the myth.[4] Such myths about solar heroes were common, not only in ancient Greece but in other antique cultures as well: the cult of the sun god Ra was widespread in Egypt in 2400 B.C., during the Fifth Dynasty. The opposition between life and death and the powers of light and darkness was particularly emphatic in the cosmological conceptions of ancient Egypt. Egyptians believed that when the night comes, the powerful Sun sets out to fight his brother, the incarnation of evil, who turns into a gigantic snake of dusk and darkness during the night. When the morning arrives, the world receives a message proclaiming the victory of goodness over evil.[5] Persian mythology contains the same irreconcilable oppositions: Ahriman, the power of darkness, and Ahura Mazda, the god of light. It is known that in Egypt Horus (as Osiris was initially called) is referred to as the "light of the world," "the Lord of life and light"; strikingly, almost identical descriptions were later used in references to the Christian God.[6] The sun was worshiped in many other Eastern civilizations: Babylonia, Asir, Persia, Phoenicia, and Asia Minor. In most ancient religions the East was associated with ideas of life and renewal, with light and warmth, while the West was associated with cold, decay and death. Graves and sanctuaries were erected taking these two poles into consideration. The great temple of Amon-Ra and the temple of Ra-Hor-Akhty at Karnak were both pointing to the mid-winter solstice sunrise.[7] Christianity probably adopted this tradition from Eastern cultures; even later Christian churches were built so that the main altar of the church was directed eastwards.[8] This was especially noted by Honorius of Autun, the author of the twelfth century's *Christian Guide to Symbols*, who wrote in his treatise: "Churches are directed to the East, where the sun rises, because in them the sun of justice is worshiped and it is foretold that it is in the east that Paradise our home is set."[9]

Pre-Socratic Greek philosophers contemplated the nature of things and attempted to single out the primary elements of the world's constitution. They classified these elements according to the degree of hardness

4. Ibid., 112–13.
5. Goldsmith, *Ancient Pagan Symbols*, 78.
6. Bayley, *Lost Language of Symbolism*, 160.
7. Merkur, *Gnosis*, 117.
8. Whittick, *Symbols*, 134.
9. Harvey, *The Medieval Architect*, 226.

or mobility. The bodiless nature of light was opposed to the tangibility of earth. The Pythagoreans, an esoteric sect that followed the vows of secrecy, were strongly influenced by the dualistic concept of morality that originated in the Orphic religion; they viewed the world as a mixture of controversial principles of good and evil, form and chaos, boundary and vagueness, and light and darkness, and believed an understanding of cosmic harmony finally leads to inner harmony, i.e., the harmony of the soul. On the other hand, Heraclitus, who objected to the Pythagorean understanding of the Cosmos, claimed that fire is the origin of all things: it destroys and provides life as if it were an eternal go-between, establishing a unity among disappearing and reappearing forms.[10]

In Egyptian hieroglyphics, fire was associated with the solar symbolism of flame, and especially with ideas of life and health. In primitive cultures fire was treated as a creative power that is radiated by the sun and is expressed by sun rays and lightning. Persian mythology contains a prophecy claiming that the world will be destroyed by either fire or water. The writings of the philosophers known as the Stoics, as well as the predictions of the Sibyls, are full of references to fire's power of purification and renewal. Plato in *Timaeus* speaks of fire, and associates it with light and the power of vision; he also insightfully notes that light is closely related to the human mind: reasoning needs light, and the light becomes visible only because it is comprehended by reason. Plotinus, the father of Neoplatonic thought, emphasized the transcendental character of light. In his philosophy, light and radiance were attributed to the one and the same source—an immaterial substance that has the power to radiate beauty, goodness, and wisdom to the material world.

THE MEDIEVAL METAPHYSICS OF LIGHT

Somewhat later, these ideas were echoed in Christian sources, especially in the writings of St. Augustine, who set out to adjust the legacy of pre-Christian thinking to the comparatively young tradition of Christian religious philosophy: his interpretation of light was based on the assumption that it is a heavenly gift to a human being, whose intelligent soul rejoices as soon as it is touched by the bodiless light.[11] Augustine's doctrine based on the divinity of light had a strong response in the

10. Cirlot, *Dictionary of Symbols*, 105.
11. Saint Augustine, *The City of God*, 299–300.

imagination of the Middle Ages, which was deeply rooted in the height of religious feeling. The celebration of the life of the senses was strongly pierced with a religious sensibility; the whole epoch was marked with the strife of searching for the invisible hand of Almighty Creator, not only in abstract values but in all things of material world. Inspired by Biblical texts, Christian philosophers and theologians stressed the duality of the phenomenon of light. In the Book of Genesis it is said that when God created the world, on the first day he separated light from darkness, and called light day and the darkness night, but it was only on the fourth day of creation that he lit the lights in the emptiness of the sky. This approach implied that light and its source were something different. The divinity of light's substance became of utmost importance in the dogmas of early Christianity; this explains why the Roman Christian Church condemned the Manichean heresy. The Manicheans, following the teaching of the Zoroastrian and Babylonian sages, preached that there was an ongoing fight between the two incompatible essences: Darkness, reigning in the material world (*Angra Mainyu* according to Zoroaster) and Light (*Spenta Mainyu*), ruling in the spiritual world. It is also important to note that in the interpretations of Holy Scripture during the early Christian period, the phenomenon and its name were closely related to one another. The name was something much more than a verbal shell enveloping the meaning. According to the medieval thinker Fridugis, who was a disciple of Alcuin, a renowned monk from York who supervised the education program initiated by Charlemagne (Fridugis was the one who eventually took over St. Martin's abbey in Tours), "day signifies light and light is something grand. The day also exists and is something grand."[12] Étienne Gilson, discussing philosophy of Johannes Scotus Eriugena, insightfully pointed out that this medieval thinker associated the notion of creation with an understanding of "illumination." Eriugena, along with other medieval thinkers, grounded his concept on the authority of the Bible, and in his comprehension nature is understood as light provided to the world and man by the supernatural powers of God. He insisted that the world would no longer continue its existence if God chose to stop radiating light.[13]

---

12. Fridugis, "Letter on Nothing and Darkness," 107.
13. Gilson, *History of Christian Philosophy*, 120.

In the twelfth century, Hugh of St. Victor, relying on Biblical sources, contemplated the nature of light. Commenting on the act of Creation, Hugh noted that

> Therefore, God, in beginning to accomplish His works made light first, that afterwards he might make all things in light. For He signified to us that he does not like works which are done in darkness, because they are evil. . . . Therefore, He himself who was to do truth, did not wish to work in darkness, but He came to light and made light, that He might make himself manifest through light.[14]

Hugh treated light as a transcendental medium through which God proclaimed his existence in heaven and on earth. Hugh firmly believed that light comes before illumination, basing this on the primacy of the law before grace, the primacy of the word before spirit, and continuing:

> Thus the law preceded grace; the word, spirit; thus John as precursor, Christ; light, light; a lamp, the sun; and Christ himself first showed His humanity, that the night thereafter make manifest this divinity; and everywhere light precedes light; the light which illuminates sinners to justice, that light which illuminates the justified to the blessedness. Therefore, light was made before the brightness of the sun was made manifest...[15]

The importance of light in Christian philosophy is echoed in the hymn composed by St. Ambrose, one of the earliest composers of this genre:

> *Splendor of paternal glory,*
> *From light radiating light.*
> *Light of light, the spring of illumination*
> *The day bringing light to the days.*[16]

St. Bonaventure, who gave so much attention to the concept of light in his writings, drew a distinction between different dimensions of light. According to Bonaventure, no matter whatever knowledge and light comes from above, from, as he puts it, "that Fountain of Light," one can distinguish the exterior light (the one of mechanical arts), interior light (philosophical knowledge), and the light of grace and the Holy

---

14. Hugh of St. Victor, *On Sacraments of Christian Faith*, 14.
15. Ibid., 17.
16. Ladner, *God, Cosmos, and Humankind*, 84.

Scripture. The light that enables us to distinguish forms of visible reality is a "light of sense perceptions" and accordingly should be called a lower one. The highest light is the one that "leads to the things above by the manifestation of truths which are beyond human reason and it is not acquired by human research, but comes down by inspiration given by 'The Father of Lights.'"[17] This notion was most probably borrowed from the writings of Dionysius the Areopagite, known as Pseudo-Dionysius, a fifth-century Syrian monk who glorified the Almighty, referring to him as *Pater Luminus*. St. Bonaventure's doctrine equated light to truth, and truth was believed to be the essence of all things. The same attitude was characteristic of Robert Grosseteste (1245), who claimed that "light is truly the principle of all beauty."[18]

And yet theoretical knowledge about the source of light and its forms was still rather limited. Johan Huizinga has drawn our attention to the fact that in speculations about beauty, notions of measure, refinement, order, grandeur, and purposefulness prevailed during the late medieval period, and thinkers were delighted in shining and light.[19] Umberto Eco has also noted that in both practice and theory, the medieval attraction to light is characterized by its directness and simplicity; however, he finds striking the obvious contradictions of this world outlook: despite the admiration of the luster of visible things, no other period in cultural history has managed to perfect a form of art in which the shining of colors merges with the luster of light.[20] This form of art is, of course, the stained glass of medieval cathedrals.

LIGHT IN MEDIEVAL ARCHITECTURE

Medieval cathedrals—the highest achievement of the civilization of the West's Middle Ages—are renowned for their special use of light and lighting. According to the metaphysical tradition of Christianity, light was employed for the purpose of creating a special spiritual atmosphere for prayer and contemplation, to shift the attention of a believer from earthly discontents to a dimension permeated by the divine spirit. The spectacular effects of colors entering the cathedral through large blocks

---

17. Saint Bonaventure, *Works*, 27.
18. Cited in Heller, "Light as Glamour," 945.
19. Huizinga, *Viduramžių ruduo*, 342.
20. Eco, *Art and Beauty*, 44.

of stained glass and the holy images drawn on the glass were to lead to the salvation of the soul. This goal was aided by all possible elements of light, shade, and color. The British architectural historian William Lethaby has noted that the miraculous, fairy-tale-like architecture, the glimmering of stained glass, the power of the sound of church bells together with organ music—all of these elements contributed to the most wonderful drama among many other dramas—that of medieval faith.[21] The plates of stained glass performed a particularly important role in the interiors of medieval cathedrals. Although there is no precise historical data pointing to precisely when stained glass began to be used in Christian sacred architecture, there is sufficient knowledge to allow the conclusion that it was widely used as early as the ninth century. One piece of evidence is a letter of Munster's bishop dated the year 846, in which he mentions a commission of stained glass. In another, Adalbert, bishop of Rheims Cathedral, mentions in his correspondence that he had ordered *fenestrisdiversas continentibus historias* (windows with various histories) for the church of St. Remigius. Thus it can be fairly concluded that during this particular period stained glass in Christian architecture was no novelty: most of the larger European churches were covered with glass during the eleventh century.[22] Early glass had an even (smooth) surface. Windows rich in color were produced, and, as Lewis Mumford has emphasized, they soon became so picturesque that the most refined Baroque carvings and gildings could hardly compete with them in terms of beauty. The workshops established in Murano in the vicinity of Venice were especially famous for the quality of their stained glass production. They produced glass for both windows and chandeliers used in ships. Though it is well known how fiercely the Venetian masters attempted to keep the knowledge of their craft a secret in order to stop any possible competition, the interest in glass-producing technologies was so strong and overwhelming that these technologies soon spread all over Italy as well as other European countries. A guild of glass makers was established in Nuremberg, Germany as early as 1373, and afterwards organizations of stained glass masters established themselves in many far-away peripheral regions of medieval Europe.[23]

21. Lethaby, *Architecture*, 207.
22. Brown, *Stained Glass*, 12–13.
23. Mumford, *Technics and Civilization*, 124.

The mystical dimension of light appeared in the art of Eastern Christianity's domain earlier than it made its appearance in Western art. Byzantine mosaics were the first art works containing the mystical dimension of light; they radiated transcendental supernatural light, and there is no doubt that the artists of the Western Christian Church largely followed these examples by employing the power of light for signification of the symbols of divinity and God's presence, and for the expression of other spiritual meanings. Sensibility toward mystic feelings was inherent to the arrangement of light effects in the sanctuaries of Eastern Christianity, where the surfaces of interior spaces concentrated and reflected the light that entered through the opening of the cupola. The mystic meanings of light manifested themselves in the architecture of Islamic cultures no less than it did in Christian sacred buildings. The mihrab of Cordoba's mosque (875–987) is a tiny room with no windows. Its half-darkness is reminiscent not of a dark bay, but of a mysterious opening to the source of a divine being surrounded by darkness.[24] However, the divinity of light manifested its full beauty in art and architecture during the later Gothic era.

Theological treatises in the Romanesque and Gothic period reveal an attempt to associate the construction of a church with liturgy. Sculptures and stained glass windows became visible illustrations of the sacred mass. The religious thinker of the thirteenth century Gulielmus Durantis, alias William Durandus, the bishop of Mende, in his treatise *Rationale Divinorum Officiorum* interpreted a church as a structure that represents the parts of a human body, where each of the sections has one or more meanings.

The glass windows of a church were explained as divine writings that protect its interior from wind and rain, but allow the real light of the sun and God to enter the church and the hearts of believers gathered for the church service. The windows of the church symbolized hospitality and compassion.[25] Besides, Durantis held that they also symbolized bodily sensations, which ought to be shut to the vanities of the world and open to receive spiritual gifts with all its freedom. To Durantis, the Gothic partition of the church window had its own explanation as well: "By the lattice work of the windows, we understand the prophets or other obscure teachers of the Church Militant; in which windows there

24. Grabar, "Architecture and Art," 154.
25. Taylor, *The Medieval Mind*, 107.

are often two shafts, signifying the two percepts of charity, or because the Apostles were sent out to preach two and two."[26]

Another important source for the medieval understanding of light was presented by Abbot Suger, the builder and author of the iconographic program of the Bernardine monastery of St. Denis—the most important French religious center during the medieval period, where the roads of pilgrims met and the bodies of France's royal rulers were buried. Following the mystical doctrine of Dionysius the Areopagite, Christian church-builders adopted his central idea that the whole creation of God is light that illuminates the mind, and the closer one is drawn to the light, the closer one moves to the Creator (and he is the true and pure light, *Lux Vera,* as the Gospel of St. John puts it). He developed a theological theory of beauty that was to be embodied in the visual forms and images of his building. Suger firmly believed that when the naves with their glass windows would be completed (alas, they were never in fact completed), adding to the choir, the final structure of the building would impersonate the one and only statement: "Light us the one that is lightly paired with light, as light is a noble building that pours onto (covers) us with a new light [*lux nova*]."[27] *Lux nova* was, of course, a biblical allusion to the Creator, who was called the God of Light. Erwin Panofsky draws our attention to another important text by Suger—a poem in which the abbot explains the meaning of the bronze door reliefs of the portal of St. Denis: "Light is a noble work, but being nobly light the work has to enlighten minds so that they could travel through true lights in the Truest Light where Christ is a true door."[28] Although Suger was unable to finish his program of decoration, one can imagine what a glorious final result was anticipated when watching the light pouring through the pure colors of glass. The stained glass of St. Denis attracted the attention of other cathedral builders, and was a constant source of inspiration throughout the Gothic period. Bearing in mind the concepts of Suger and his numerous followers, it is no wonder that Gothic cathedrals became magnificent visible incarnations of teachings that glorified light's and God's presence in Christian sanctuaries. The streams of light pouring into cathedrals through windows that symbolized the divine scriptures brought daylight into their interiors as well as God into the

26. Durantis, *Symbolism,* 28–29.
27. Cunningham and Reich, *Culture and Values,* 183.
28. Panofsky, *Meaning in Visual Arts,* 164.

hearts of believers. The invention of stained glass and its application in architecture gave a powerful impetus to make Gothic cathedrals true sanctuaries of light, transforming abstract ideas and concepts into an impressive visible medium that bespoke the presence of God. Gothic architecture was a remarkable, almost unsurpassable embodiment of the spiritual powers of light, never to be equaled in any other epoch in cultural history, never mind during our own period with its lack of respect for traditional wisdom and spiritual experience.

The quality of color in Gothic stained glass is amazing. The technique of creating the luxuriant red and blue colors of Chartres cathedral remains something of a mystery even today, especially since even the application of the most advanced modern technologies are unable to adequately recreate them. Another aspect testifying to the importance of stained glass in the Christian sanctuaries of this period is the size and number of windows. For example, in Chartres Cathedral there are as many as 173 openings covered with glass, making up a total of 1672 square meters. No wonder that so many visitors to this remarkable architectural structure are overwhelmed by the intensity of its colors and lights. Even scholars can hardly restrain their feelings while describing the aesthetic qualities of Gothic stained glass. This is evident from the text of James Rosser Johnson, who notes:

> In the nave of Chartres no extraneous light is allowed to break the spell. The heavily saturated reds and blues glow uninterruptedly in a low-keyed atmosphere created by deep translucent colors infinitely varied in hue, yet carefully ordered within a harmonious scale of intensities. A mood is established by shielding out all natural light, thereby transforming the vast interior into a mysterious region of shadowy form and glowing color. The eye perceives no surface illumination defining boundaries or revealing the physical function of glazed enclosures; rather, one receives an impression of softly diffused, unbounded luminosity 'pervading the interior beauty' transforming all things.[29]

The shape, hues, and technique of producing stained glass changed with time. The glass gradually became lighter and more transparent; more and more varied hues were added to the prevailing color scheme. Meanwhile, the red color became more lustrous and lost its former transparency, and blue became more and more like purple and green. There were sig-

---

29. Johnson, *Radiance of Chartres*, 15–16.

nificant changes in the images in the stained glass windows as well: the scenes acquired a didactic or educational character.

In the fourteenth century, these changes became especially visible: the colors of the stained glass lost their glitter, white or monochromic plates of glass were used much more often, the frames of windows were treated architecturally, and the figures chosen for representation depended on the architectural composition of the drawing. By the end of that century white glass was dominant; all other colors were of much lesser importance. Transparent glass let such large quantities of light into the interiors of cathedrals that the figures depicted in the windows appear to be evaporating in the air.[30] The relation between light and religious symbolism so important in the late medieval period was perfectly summarized by Rudolf Arnheim, who wrote that

> As radiation of divine light, the light becomes a natural part of religious architecture. The light makes its way through the windows without breaking the glass, and this feature was understood as a sign of its spirituality; when the pure light of the sun was disseminated into different colorful earthly pictures by the stained glass, it symbolized a neoplatonic doctrine, which claims that the heavenly light gradually overcomes the darkness of physical world.[31]

However, some scholars are inclined to question the thesis that the relationship between light and interior spaces is the essence of medieval architecture. Architectural historian and theorist Paul Frankl is one of the main defenders of this attitude. He claimed that the metaphysics of light, symbolism, the cult of the carts, and crusades do not explain Gothic any more than Gothic explains those phenomena. Frankl continues: "They all, however, have their common roots in the heightened religious fervor of that generation. Gothic architecture expressed in its language what was taking place in those other intellectual fields. For art is form as the expression, or, more precisely, the symbol of the spiritual content inherited in form or in other intellectual spheres."[32]

---

30. Aubert, *Art of the High Gothic*, 109.
31. Arnheim, *The Split and the Structure*, 80.
32. Frankl, *The Gothic*, 23.

BETWEEN SACRUM AND PROFANUM

The concept of the divinity of light was cherished until the very end of the Middle Ages. One can find its reflection in the treatises of Renaissance Christian thinkers as well. The Christian mystic Katherine of Genoa (1447–1511) claimed that the light of God enlightens a human soul in one instant, and also that the human mind can not define it.[33] This statement meant that the knowledge provided by enlightenment does not depend on the powers of human mind; it is awarded by God, who chooses the human being to whom he wishes to give his grace. The Neoplatonists of the Renaissance revived interest in the metaphysical problems of light in their own way, drawing on non-Christian as well as Christian sources. One of the spiritual leaders of this revival of Platonic thought, Marcilio Ficino, revived the Egyptian cult of the sun and disseminated it among Italian humanists, whose minds were wide open to the spiritual and mental legacy of antiquity. He interpreted the sun as an order that descends upon the earth from the heavens as both God and Divine Light. Other thinkers of the Renaissance made their own contribution to the understanding of light. Leonardo da Vinci, in a treatise on painting that was published long after the artist's death, contemplated the essence of light. However, he was less interested in its metaphysical aspects than in its physical ones. Leonardo claimed that the human eye is a perfect instrument of vision that opens the beauty of the world to human sight, and that to lose vision means to imprison the human soul. The color white, according to Leonardo, represented the very light; and without it no other light can be envisioned. As far as light reveals the quality of colors, its value can be best observed where the light is best. Meanwhile dark bodies can be lightened in four ways: universal (daylight): specific (when the object is brought to light by sun through a window or an open door); by reflection; and diffusion, when the light penetrates through a light material (e.g., linen or paper). Leonardo wrote: "the lighting rises from the being of light and shining is a reflection of this light."[34] It can be noted in this context that it was due to those Renaissance theorists who built their doctrines on the importance of white that transparent, translucent glass started to prevail in the architectural structures of this period.

33. Hügel, *The Mystical Element*, 270–71.
34. Leonardo, *On Painting*, 90.

The metaphysical aspects of light and lighting were discussed long after the end of the Renaissance; however, artists and architects more and more often discussed technical aspects of light without association or links to the tradition of metaphysical thinking. Despite the decline of metaphysics, the art of stained glass continued to flourish in Rome throughout the Renaissance. This was something of a paradox, or at least an anachronism, as the development of the aesthetics of stained glass was mainly due to the efforts of a single man—Pope Julius II, who was a guardian of the masters who created stained glass windows. This might be somewhat surprising—that this Pope of truly Renaissance spirit was so faithful to outdated medieval aesthetics—but one can understand the sympathies of the Pope as loyalty to beauty, richness of color, and glamour, which he shared with many of his predecessors and heirs.[35]

The changes in the use of lighting in architectural structures of the later epochs was predetermined not by metaphysical or religious causes, but by the practical demands of everyday life and the technological advancements that made these changes possible. By the sixteenth century, the pointed arch in European architecture was replaced with the much more practical flat arch and a square window. These architectural and structural innovations demanded a new arrangement of interior lighting. Since the height of spaces in these buildings was limited, larger windows provided better conditions for interior lighting.[36] On the other hand, the development of production technologies lowered the cost of glass; consequently, glass became affordable not only to the richest individuals, but to people of other social strata as well. Only the southern countries, because of their specific climate, failed to follow this trend. By the end of the eighteenth century, because of advancements in the technological sphere and the constantly diminishing costs of glass, window frames were constructed sufficiently larger to allow more light inside buildings.

Thus metaphysical notions that had dominated for several millenniums gave way to more practical building considerations. And yet, one should not forget that throughout the entire history of human civilization, almost all religious and philosophical doctrines underlined the metaphysical aspects and origins of light and its relation to divine sources. For some time after the waning of the Renaissance, a metaphysical interpretation of light continued to exist with almost no significant

---

35. Wohl, *Aesthetics of Italian Renaissance Art*, 199.
36. Foster, *Principles of Architecture*, 153.

changes; it was still related to divinity, however, the new scientific world outlook was taking over the old metaphysical thinking. The scientific revolution in the seventeenth century began to dismantle the foundations of metaphysical religious thinking as scientists turned their eyes to the physical structure of nature. The endeavor to understand the essence of natural phenomena with the help of scientific inquiry urged experimentation instead of speculation. Experimental research of the physical world slowly but assuredly paved the way for a positivistic analysis of the phenomenology of light. Kenneth Clark has convincingly demonstrated how deeply the greatest minds of that century were preoccupied with the natural sciences: Spinoza was renowned not only as the greatest thinker of Netherlands, but also one of the best producers of lenses in Europe; the philosopher Descartes carried out important research on the phenomena of refraction; and Huygens developed a theory of waves.[37]

There was another line of thinking as well. An ordinary cobbler named Jacob Boehme "was struck by the divine light" one day in the year 1600 while contemplating the essence of things, and eventually became one of the greatest theosophic thinkers of that century. It was this mystic who had a huge impact on the Newtonian theory of gravitation and research on the structure of light; in the same way, much later, his treatises on the supernatural origin of light became sources of inspiration to the critics of Newton, such as Wolfgang Johann Goethe and William Blake. According to Boehme, the human soul is an eye of fire or its mirror, through which God reveals himself to a man; meanwhile darkness hides in the center of light, and everyone who attempts to ignore the Almighty finally finds himself in burning flames, in the same fire through which Lucifer entered. Boehme insisted that fire is the original existence of the soul, and fire is its life, but if the soul does not leave darkness and enter the light with the help of will and imagination, as if passing through a dreadful death into another principle—that of Fire-Love—it remains in its original fire.[38] His mystical concepts remained attractive to many other thinkers who chose to find explanations not with the help of experimental science, but with the older tradition of metaphysical inquiry into the nature of things and mystical revelations. It is no wonder that centuries later the Russian theosophic thinker Nikolai Berdyaev bowed to a person he considered his great predecessor. According to Berdyaev,

37. Clark, *Civilization*, 212.
38. Roob, *Alchemy and Mysticism*, 253.

Jacob Boehme was one of the first minds to understand the life of the cosmos as a passionate fight, as movement, process, and eternal resurrection. And it was Jacob Boehme, the autodidactic mystic, who provided far-reaching insights into the elliptical orbits of planets before Johannes Kepler, and whose writings gave an impetus to future scientists to discover the secret of the spectrum. Robert Fludd (1574–1637), another mystic of that period, defender of the mysterious order of the Rosicrucians, argued that the divine act of creation was similar to an alchemic process, during which God educed three primary elements out of the chaos—light, darkness, and spiritual waters. These three elements were the source of the four essential elements indicated by Aristotle. Fludd's writings were embedded in the idea of light's divine origin. The light was interpreted as an active rudiment that enabled the divine act of creation to be carried out: when the light of God descended from the heights and illuminated the chaos, and chaos was thus organized into visible forms, these forms gave birth to the world. When the light met chaos, water came into being—the most dynamic substance. During this process water was divided into two parts: the heavenly and the earthly, and the earthly one was divided into the spheres of air, water, and earth. Fludd concluded that the mass of humid water could be reduced to an object of pyramid shape. And "so also the mass of light in the world streaming from the presence of God shining out of darkness may be reduced into a formal pyramid's encountridge in his descent the material on ascending upwards in an equal proportion."[39] Religious mysticism followed a line of thought that had existed since antiquity, however, the tradition of metaphysical thinking and mysticism as its separate branch was gradually waning and giving way to scientific explanations of natural phenomena, a movement that characterized the arrival of the modern epoch.

LIGHT AND TRADITION IN MODERN ARCHITECTURE

On the eve of the advent of modern times, several Western philosophers attempted reconsidering the importance of light in different types of visual art. Georg Hegel insisted that objects of sculpture and architecture become visible to human eye because of light coming from the outside, while painting—which in itself is dark—contains the light inside the

---

39. Fludd, *Robert Fludd and His Philosophical Key*, 152.

material, as its own ideal.[40] Arthur Schopenhauer, the great critic of Hegel and the rationalism of Western philosophy, was one of the first to elucidate the specific relation between architecture and the phenomenon of light, despite the fact that he treated architecture as a lower form of art in comparison to music and the visual arts, on account of of its utility and usefulness. On the other hand, Schopenhauer's concept of light was influenced by his interest in Eastern philosophical sources, the Hindu Upanishads in particular. The latter spoke of the joy, blessing, and symbolism of goodness inherent to light and confirmed by all religious traditions. Schopenhauer reflected on the essence of light in the following way: light is "the biggest diamond in the crown of beauty" and it produces an essential influence on the knowledge of each object that is considered beautiful. The being of light generally is a compulsory condition, as it strengthens the beauty of almost all most beautiful objects. However, light is especially benevolent to the beauty of architecture, and because of light even the most obscure architectural object can become extremely beautiful.[41]

Schopenhauer associated the impact of light not with the human will, but with pure knowledge, and claimed that light conditions beauty in any architectural object. He suggested that architectural structures become doubly beautiful in the strong light of the sun, when they are set in the background of a blue sky, and have a different look when lit by the moon. Accordingly, anyone who wishes to erect an architectural building should first consider the effect that comes into being because of the light and the building's orientation toward separate parts of the world. It is only a strong, clear light that is able to emphasize all parts of a building and their relation to each other, and thus the art of architecture, in the same way as it reveals weight and hardness, should also reveal the essence of light, which is altogether different from those two powers. The light that enters the large, clearly delineated masses of a building as it is reflected by them, insists Schopenhauer, reveals its nature to the viewer in the most pure way, because light is a condition of perfect visual knowledge.[42]

The insights of Hegel and Schopenhauer were new in the tradition of Western philosophy and aesthetics, however, they were hardly a novelty in the architectural practices of many different cultures. Bernard

40. Cited in Arnheim, *The Split and the Structure*, 81.
41. Schopenhauer, *Pasaulis*, 295.
42. Ibid., 311–12.

Rudofsky, who was the curator of a celebrated pioneering exhibition *Architecture Without Architects* held in New York a few decades ago, has shown convincingly that the role and importance of light was well known and understood in a variety of ancient cultures that made use of natural light. The effects of lighting, acoustics, and scent merged to create the unique aesthetic feeling of a place—not a space—that often remains only a promise in the architectural shapes of contemporary cities, despite the abundance of advanced building technologies and financial means. Covered village streets in such different places as Benabarre (Spain), Gubbio (Italy), and the Kharga oasis (Libya) demonstrate remarkable visual effects of daylight hardly found in the most sophisticated contemporary architectural buildings. One can also draw on examples of traditional living architecture. In contemporary Mexican rural areas rather simple, ordinary building constructions are employed; however, they use powerful daylight effects. The corridors between parts of the building are lit from above by the sun, and the contrast of light and shade becomes visible in each part of the house. The dynamics of light, the interplay between light and darkness, as well as enclosures made of natural materials create far better lighting than any sort of artificial lighting could provide.

One can also note that there were distinguished modern architects who were extremely conscious of light effects, and employed the wisdom of traditional architecture. Frank Lloyd Wright—one of the most distinguished figures in the architecture of the twentieth century—was especially interested in the architectural legacy and building principles of ancient cultures and the traditional architecture of the East. These life-long studies had a profound influence on his concept of organic architecture, closely related to the interaction between nature and the built environment. The humanistic architectural philosophy of Frank Lloyd Wright, as well as his excellent knowledge of ancient building principles, enabled him to shed more light on the role of light and shade in nature and in the environment created by human beings, so that the luster of light together with depth of shadows open new spaces for creative thinking, and a new feeling for a place.[43] Truly democratic new architecture, he maintained, had to reconsider the principles of institutions governing life in present society, as well as the real needs of the people. This is the only means whereby architecture is able to give

---

43. Wright, *The Future of Architecture*, 235.

back to the people what the development of civilization has deprived them of: the ability to comprehend the beauty of nature, the inherent superiority of natural materials, and to develop a feeling for form, mass, and the intricate relations between vertical and horizontal lines. Among many other things, future modern architecture was destined to make human beings more sensitive to space as it is affected by light. Wright's plan for the Crystal City, transparent during the day and glistening during the night, deserves at least a passing mention. This powerful vision utilizing steel construction and glass was interpreted as a place where light, cleanliness, and security would be concentrated. Though full of admiration for ancient building traditions, Wright never despised technological progress and its challenges to architecture. He saw the difference between old and new architecture in terms of the aesthetic and functional possibilities that the advancement of technologies provided. The role of the architect was to use these possibilities to produce new aesthetic effects and dwellings that would be more comfortable and thus more human. He regretted that some modern cities, despite the significant progress of building technologies, still bear close associations with the constantly dark, wet, and uncomfortable caves of primitive man. Wright, as was quite natural in his day, held a firm belief in the future possibilities of the role of glass in architecture, seeing the connection between the spreading use of glass and the technical advances that made glass transparent, varied in quality and size, and last but not least cheap. He even noted that if humans had had these possibilities in ancient times, the history of architecture would have been very different.[44]

Frank Lloyd Wright not only meditated on the qualities of glass, but widely experimented with its application in architectural structures; it is no wonder he is often considered the initiator of indirect light in the interiors of buildings. Quite early in his career he developed an interest in reshaping the sources of light in interior spaces: the effects of lighting were modeled so that light on the floor would be projected to the ceiling, or that an opening in the ceiling would disseminate light in the niches of the walls. He proved convincingly that no matter how large interior spaces are, and no matter what their function, a large variety of visual lighting effects can be created. The Wright-designed V. S. Morris Shop in San Francisco is widely acknowledged as a masterpiece of integrated lighting; his Taliesin West contains marvelous visual effects

---

44. Wright, *On Architecture*, 122.

through the arrangement of natural light in the interior of the loggia. The role of light was given a special emphasis in his church projects: he aspired not only to provide a special atmosphere for contemplation and prayer through the symbolism of light, but also to utilize light's ability to make interiors "warmer" and more human. While commenting on the interior structure of his Unity Temple (Oak Park, Chicago), Wright wrote: "Flood these side-alcoves with light from above: get a sense of a happy cloudless day into the room. And with this feeling for light the center ceiling between the four posts became skylight, daylight sifting through amber glass ceiling lights, thus the light would, rain or shine, have the warmth of sunlight."[45]

The role of light in architecture is so essential that it can reconcile the attitudes of the most ardent aesthetic opponents. It is well known that Frank Lloyd Wright never appreciated the architectural principles and practices of Le Corbusier, another key architect of the twentieth century, who preached a megalomaniac vision of future architecture and demanded grand-scale transformations of modern metropolises. However, no matter how irreconcilable their world views were, both architects shared a feeling for light in modern architecture. In his early work Le Corbusier was mainly interested in the technical aspects of lighting. A formal system of modern architecture was presented in his treatise *Five Points for Modern Architecture* (1926), which also contained a discussion on the role of light. To contain maximum light in a room, Le Corbusier suggested "a free façade," covered by a glaze capable of reflecting light, and a long horizontal window—*la fenetre longeur*—allowing a thick stream of light to cover the interior space.[46] Unfortunately, when these recommendations were applied in practice, it turned out that despite seemingly precise calculations, these large openings proved unable to provide an adequate quality of daylight for the interior spaces. Besides, in summer such architectural structures suffered from the unpleasant hothouse effect, and in winter from large heat losses of heat because of poor insulation.[47] His failure to "orchestrate" light with the help of large openings did not stop him from further experiments; he is known to have invented a device called a *brise-soleil* to be used in southern climates, which proved to be applicable in other regions as well. But the most significant turn in

45. Wright, *Writings and Buildings*, 78.
46. Etlin, *Wright and Corbusier*, 17.
47. Banham, *Architecture*, 151–52.

his line of thinking occurred when the architect became more interested in the metaphysical aspects of light than in purely technical devices. This occurred when Le Corbusier designed the chapel of Notre-Dame-du-Haut, Ronchamp (1950–55), where he exchanged a mystery for the creation of a functional attitude. Approaching the mystical doctrines of light, he constructed the interior space of the chapel to incorporate the mysticism of light in a seemingly perfect visual form. The chapel at Ronchamp stands as a clear message that even modern and secular culture can contain spaces where light manifests itself as more than a purely physical phenomenon—spaces that express a close relationship with metaphysical notions and speak to the longing for a vertical dimension still important to many people of religious faith. The same mysterious concept of light emanates from his famous Villa Shodan, which contains many virtuoso, almost painterly light effects. Through allowing light to enter the interior of the villa through window perforations, he proved that the metaphysics of light aren't restricted to the architecture of sacred buildings, but can reappear in any human dwelling, thereby bringing another reality to the fore, that of an outside world that we will perhaps never be able to reduce to purely physical phenomena.

THE ELECTRIC BULB VERSUS SUNLIGHT

There are those who believe that the expansion of possible applications by modern technologies of artificial lighting not only conditioned a new view of spatial representation, but had a radical impact on the visual sensitivity of human beings. Such an attitude, for example, is expressed by György Képes.[48] However, this optimism is apparently somewhat misplaced, given the controversial consequences of changes introduced by new technologies of lighting. One should never forget that since time immemorial, natural daylight had the greatest impact on the comprehension of architecture and all other visual phenomena. The peculiarities of natural light, related to the duration of day and night, locality, climate, and the topography of landscape, have always been taken into consideration in modeling architectural spaces to make the best possible use of daylight. Accordingly, artificial lighting was considered secondary to natural light, and was reserved for use when the light of the sun was becoming dim and buildings were gliding into the realm of darkness. A

---

48. Képes, *The Language of Vision*, 154.

variety of distinguished modern architects had a somewhat restricted attitude towards artificial light; they rejected claims to its superiority over natural daylight, despite the difficulties inherent in controlling the latter due to its changeability. Louis I. Kahn, who had a special attitude towards daylight, occasionally meditated on the phenomena of light and silence. In a memorable passage he discusses the power of natural light:

> I look at the glancing light on the side of the mountain, which is such a meaningful light, bringing every tiny natural detail to the eye, and teaching us about material and choice in making a building. But do I get less delight out of seeing a brick wall with all its attempts at regularity, its delightful imperfections revealed in natural light? A wall is built in the hope that a light once observed may strike it again in a rare moment of time. How can anyone imagine a building of spaces not seen in natural light? Schools are being built with little or no natural light, supposedly to save on maintenance costs and to assure the teachers of their pupils' undivided attention. The most wonderful aspects of the indoors are the moods that light gives to space. The electric bulb fights the sun.[49]

Contemplating the visual impressions experienced while looking at the natural environment and buildings, the architect emphasizes the huge impact ever-changing, dynamic, and varied natural light makes on the perception of both natural and man-made artifacts. And despite the fact that the highly developed modern technologies of artificial lighting have opened wide possibilities for manipulating light, and no matter how sophisticated these technologies are, they will never provide the human mind with such astonishing, beautiful, subtle, indispensable views as natural light does. The modern addiction to technologies captivates both the vision and the mind. The entrapment of mind and vision results in an inability to feel the omnipotent presence of natural light. Kahn regretted that architects "in planning rooms today have forgotten their faith in natural light. Depending on the touch of a finger to a switch, they are satisfied with static light and forget the endlessly changing qualities of natural light, in which a room is a different room every second of the day."[50] He was one of those few exceptionally insightful Western architects who managed to resist the mass technologization of mind and retained

---

49. Kahn, "Architecture, Silence and Light," 29–30.
50. Ibid., 30.

a sensibility for natural light. In another essay, published in 1960, Kahn remarked that artificial lighting is always a static light, and therefore will never be equal to nuances of moods that are provided by the time of the day and wonders of the seasons.[51] His loyalty to natural light is evident in his architecture. Natural light is especially skillfully used in Kahn's Rochester Unitarian church: although visitors are overwhelmed by light from both sides as soon as they enter the church, they are protected from it being too intense or irritating the sight. The Christian sanctuary was designed so that opening of windows can glimmer and be overcast.[52] This careful arrangement of lighting helps to create the special meditative atmosphere that is so frequently desired but so rarely achieved in modern church buildings.

The mystical and metaphysical dimension of light, which was an indivisible part of sacred architecture for centuries, was of interest to many architects of the last century in their designs for sanctuaries of different religions and congregations. The meanings and symbolism implied in the arrangement of sources of light in the Church of Light in Osaka, Japan, designed by Tadao Ando, might, with a certain justice, be interpreted as a visual expression of the Neoplatonic doctrine of light in architectural forms. Blinding light pouring through the cruciform in the wall of the church becomes a visible manifestation of the divinity of light and the mystery of faith. Visitors are induced into a holy mystery; they seem to witness that beyond our earthly physical reality there exists another kind of being that takes shape in a stream of pure light. The same visual and sensory effect was created by Eero Saarinen, who designed the Kresge Chapel at the Massachusetts Institute of Technology. However, in the Kresge Chapel the source of light is located on the ceiling above the altar, and the light, as if a streaming flow of water, pours downwards, urging meditation, and subtly prompting a believer to metaphysical reflections and a reality that stretches far beyond the physical phenomena of light. One has the impression that the lessons given by Le Corbusier in his Ronchamp Chapel were skillfully learned by Sir Basil Spense, an architect who designed a baptistry of Covent Cathedral, where a perforated wall divides the inside space from the outside, and small openings of light create a mysterious, meditative atmosphere. Stained glass of various intensity covering these small openings allows

51. Scully, *Louis I. Kahn*, 118.
52. Ibid., 34.

very different streams of light to enter the space of the chapel: in some places the light is very distinct, while in other parts it loses its brightness and becomes more and more dim, until it gradually disappears and gives way to the overwhelming deep shadow of darkness. Architects Harrison and Abramowitz chose a different approach in designing the Stanford Presbyterian Church (Connecticut, USA): the whole building was covered by a roof made of stained glass where dark blue and red colors prevail. Thus the light enters the church from above, and the colors mingle, creating a special contemplative atmosphere. Examples of this type of construction, where light enters the interior spaces from above, are quite numerous in Christian churches designed in the last century.

Lighting problems were solved in a different way by architects designing civic buildings, who were less concerned with the symbolic meanings light carries. A perfect example of functional system lighting is the Stockholm city library, designed by the renowned Swedish architect Eric Asplund, who took great efforts to ensure that the interior spaces of the building would contain an abundance of light. He further demonstrated a skillful management of lighting in the Stockholm City Hall—a structure he designed after carefully learning from the failure of the Copenhagen City Hall, erected before he was given his own commission by the city of Stockholm. The interior spaces of the Copenhagen City Hall, despite the fact that they were lit from above (the whole ceiling of one of its halls is a source of light) proved to lack character and expression; there was a lack of the interplay between light and darkness that gives life to interior and exterior spaces alike. Asplund decided not to use the ceiling for the window openings; instead he placed windows in the upper part of the wall, close to the ceiling. Accordingly, the interior lighting turned out to be clearer and more transparent, and the reading hall more comfortable and usable for a longer part of the day without artificial lighting. Asplund was well aware that a transparent roof used as a cavity to let the light in is not the best solution at all. Far better effects can be created by placing the windows at the upper part of the walls and lighting the space from several sides.

New problems surfaced with the development of artificial lighting. One should not forget that cities and towns remained in total darkness at night for several millennia, up until the advent of the nineteenth century. When streets were finally lit at night, first gas, and then electricity was employed to do so. As a result, city buildings became visible not just in daylight, as in the olden days. According to Per Stounberg, this radical novelty gave impetus to a number of changes: metaphors of light acquired a new basis, and artificial lighting not only changed the way of life of city dwellers, but made a huge impact on the understanding of a city, on its visual symbolism.[53] Of course those individuals who prefer a "city that never sleeps" as a symbol of the contemporary city will in any case give pride and glory to metropolitan metaphors built on technological innovations. Illuminated by electricity, large modern cities, or more precisely, megalopolises, became symbols of glimmering luxury, dynamism, and a busy night life. However, the glamor of city lights casts a shadow on many not-so-subtle nuances and contradictions of contemporary urban life, and on our understanding of the city as a product of civilization. The growing impact of artificial lighting on the human mind and the problems this presented was noted by Reyner Banham:

> Electric lighting thus put the challenge of environmental technology to architects in direct terms of the art of architecture, because the sheer abundance of light, in conjunction with large areas of transparent or translucent material, effectively reversed all established visual habits by which the buildings were seen. And this possibility was realized and exploited without the support of any corpus of theory adapted to the new circumstances, or even of a workable vocabulary for describing these visual effects and their environmental consequences. No doubt this accounts for the numerous failures in this century to produce the effects and environments desired . . .[54]

It would be unjust to claim that contemporary architects were blinded by the overwhelming possibilities of lighting technologies and gave up their loyalty to natural light and its elusive character. Some Western architects were very sensitive to the new conditions for lighting and adequately realized the changes it brought to the rhythm of contemporary city life, neither ignoring daylight nor turning back to the abundance of uses that artificial lighting provides. These architects were concerned with how their buildings would look like both during the daytime and at night. For example, Eric Mendelsohn is known to have designed sketches for the night lighting of his architectural buildings.

---

53. Stounberg, "The Overexposed City," 185.
54. Banham, *Architecture*, 70.

And yet no matter how advanced and sophisticated the recent lighting technologies have become, and despite changes in the life rhythm of city dwellers, most buildings are still seen and perceived in natural light throughout the day. According to renowned Danish architect and architectural theorist Steen Eiler Rasmussen, daylight in architecture is the most dynamic, least determined element, which is extremely difficult to subject to the architect's control. Turning his attention to natural lighting, Rasmussen classified its varieties into three most common "paradigmatic" types (though the term paradigm does not belong to his original vocabulary): the first one being a light open room; the second, a closed room lit from above; and the third one, a room of mixed types of lighting in various combinations. Construction of the first type usually prevails in regions with a warm climate, i.e., Southern cultures; the second dominates in Northern countries; and the most extraordinary example of the third type of lighting were Dutch historical interiors. Since Dutch town dwellers were conscious of the cost of each square meter, they erected houses set side by side, and usually used the upper floor to store their goods, so only the façade windows of the ground floor could be used for light. Deprived of natural means, they utilized tiny window openings to the utmost, with the help of shutters and curtains, so as to let more light into their long narrow rooms.

Meanwhile, one can only agree with Rasmussen that the Pantheon in Rome is an unsurpassed example of an architectural structure where the closed room is lit from above. The carefully calculated proportion of the dome and the harmoniously balanced interior volumes have an impact upon lighting effects, and the light pouring from the opening above melts into the space without leaving even the smallest place for deep shadows. He also draws our attention to the fact that when structures attempted to emulate the Pantheon, even the slightest changes in its proportions resulted in failure.[55] Thus, having in mind these exceptional creations of human genius, one is inclined to conclude that our present belief in repeatable, changeable, reproducible objects is shaken by some of world's most distinguished architectural structures.

---

55. Rasmussen, *Experiencing Architecture*, 186.

SUMMING UP

Metaphysical and religious-philosophic concepts have been reflected in architectural structures since the very beginnings of this art, and are closely related to the nature of architecture. Testimonies about the influence of cosmological world views on architecture can be found in historical cultures of both the ancient East and West. The bonds between metaphysical doctrines and architecture are especially apparent in antiquity. The cosmology of the Pythagoreans and the analogies between mathematic and music discovered by the founders of this esoteric tradition were applied in architecture for over two millennia. Pythagorean ideas merged into the metaphysical doctrines of Christianity, and emerged in new shapes during the Middle Ages and Renaissance.

The metaphysical notions of light that influenced the development of Christian architecture reached their climax of expression during the late Middle Ages. However, the various concepts of divinity of light manifested in Islamic architecture demonstrate that the origins of these doctrines are related to the much older heritage of eastern cosmology. With the rise and development of the scientific world view and scientific research into optics in the post-Renaissance period, the metaphysical aspect of light gradually lost its former prominence. The growth of the scientific world view and technological advancement interrupted the continuity of metaphysical conceptions, and essentially transformed the notion of sacredness associated with light and its relation to architecture. The utmost rationality of the Enlightenment moved the tradition of esoteric knowledge to the margins of Western culture. However, the ambiguous developments of modernity gave sufficient ground for dissatisfaction with the cult of reason, rationality, and ideas of technological progress. This dissatisfaction gave impetus to modern thinkers and architects alike to reconsider the legacy of Western thinking shaped by post-Renaissance tendencies in general, and by the Enlightenment in particular. These attempts to reconsider the lost tradition of metaphysical thinking and the "vertical" dimension of spirituality can be seen in some works of modern architecture.

2

Architecture and Color

There is an account of a conversation between two simple boys in a nineteenth-century novel. One of them is trying to envision a world without any colors whatsoever, and asks his friend about the possibility. His companion, apparently less endowed with imagination, cannot comprehend such an idea—in fact he suspects that the other boy has simply gone out of his mind. No matter which interpretation one chooses, one thing is obvious: it is difficult to imagine a real world with no colors at all. Nature itself has provided us with the experience of color, and only a person deprived of the inborn ability to see colors could object to a world perceived as containing an innumerable variety of them.

This story forces us to consider the significance of the phenomenon of color in a visual world. Color, in the same way as light, is one of the most fundamental, most essential sources of visual experiences, enriching human life with a pleasure that only variety can provide. Color is such an obvious, undeniable, and inseparable part of our environment that we take it as something granted, something obvious in its own right, something that exists naturally and does not even demand any special contemplation or explanation. It exists everywhere in nature, opening itself to human sight and spontaneously urging us to experience a vast number of psychophysical and aesthetic reactions—from utmost awe to a sense of disgust. No wonder the French modernist painter Fernand Leger has so justly and insightfully remarked that the lust for color is as natural to a human being as his or her need for water and fire.[1]

---

1. Leger, "On Monumentality," 40.

The human sensitivity to color is substantiated by prehistoric drawings found in caves, drawings made by using natural materials that our ancestors found in their environment. There is no doubt that in this period of the infancy of the human race, the sense for nature was already highly developed in human beings, in as much as it was associated with an inborn instinct to survive in a world full of powers far exceeding the ones possessed by our prehistoric ancestors. The sharp eye of a primitive man—a hunter, which allowed him to notice the subtlest shades of the skin of a wild animal, as well as a naturally developed feeling for smell, provided a human being with more opportunities to survive in a wild and dangerous environment and to continue his own species. As time went by, color was used to decorate the primitive hut of a prehistoric human being. As we know today, naturally colored materials were adopted initially, but eventually human beings learned how to produce more varied colors by mixing different ingredients and expanding their knowledge of paint and colors, as well as their possible combinations. It is worth noting that various red, black, brown, and yellow color shades are found in the oldest cave drawings; however, such colors as green, blue, or white were never used. Only later did humans learn how to procure these colors.[2] Different natural colors were used in each region, depending on local conditions, climate, and the available materials most easily extracted and used for decoration. To this very day, every culture, especially its provincial settlements, contains specific color schemes that depend on local traditions and building materials.

THE ARCHAIC METAPHYSICS OF COLOR

Perhaps one of the first among the known attempts to understand the nature of color from a theoretical point of view can be found in the ancient source of Hindu philosophy, the *Upanishads* (seventh to eighth century B.C.). The color red was associated with fire, white with water, black with the earth, and all the unknown colors were explained as combinations of these three. Written sources from other archaic cultures also contain meditations on the making of color. The thinkers of ancient Greece attempted to comprehend the problem of the origin of color as part of the structure of the world and the cosmos. In *Timaeus*, Plato calls color a fire that flows from every body. He set out to explain the process,

---

2. Pastoreau, *Blue: The History of a Color*, 13.

claiming that particles flowing from other bodies meet the ray of sight, and colors are perceived because they are either smaller, bigger, or the same size as those that constitute the ray. Accordingly, particles of the same size are not sensed, and because of that they are called invisible or transparent; meanwhile, those that are bigger clasp it, and those that are smaller enlarge it. Thus their influence upon sight can be compared to the effect of cold or heat on our body, as well as the effect of sweet or sour on the tongue. According to Plato, glistering colors come into being because of the encounter of two fires. However, he claimed that there is another kind of fire that reaches the humidity of the eye and mixes with it. The twinkling of this fire as it enters through the liquid becomes the color red. When fire mixes with red or white, the color yellow results. The blending of red with black and white produces purple or dark violet. When yellow gets mixed with gray, it creates the color brown.[3] This explanation of the origin of color, taken in the context of the sophisticated Greek philosophical thought of the period as well as Plato's own musings on other subjects, seems rather simplistic and too mechanical. It is obvious that meditations on the origin of color in Plato's philosophy do not correspond to his far more deeply developed ideas about the origin and structure of other things, for example light, sound, or harmony. In *Philebus*, Plato's discussion of color is much more subtle: he claims that colors produce the same kind of pleasure as sounds and smells, and that these things are beautiful absolutely rather than relatively.[4] To put it otherwise, he insists that pure colors or hues give pleasure to the human eye in and of themselves, no matter how big or small they are, or in what proportions they exist. However, in *The Republic*, Plato notes that despite the human gift of vision and his contention that things have color in order that our eyes can see them, still another element is needed. This important third element is light.[5]

Aristotle claimed that colors come into being when darkness meets light, and darkness springs from the non-existence of light. He distinguished seven basic colors that are extracted when two opposites—white and black—meet each other.[6] Yellow, red, purple, green, and blue are positioned in between these two extremes. The most pleasurable color is

---

3. Plato, *Timaeus*, 68.
4. Plato, "From *Philebus*," 30.
5. Plato, *The Republic*, 218.
6. Aristotle, *Works*, 264.

attained when the proportion of black and white in the mixture is equal to 3:2 or 3:4. Thus, according to Aristotle, a simple ratio creates colors that provide pleasure (he mentions purple and dark red as examples) in the same way as harmonies in music do; meanwhile, irrational proportions create colors that lack purity and are consequently less beautiful.

Pliny, following Aristotle, identified three basic colors: red, purple, and violet. Later Plotinus, who rejected the widespread doctrine that claimed the beauty of visible images is created by the balance of its parts together with its colors, insisted that there are things whose beauty does not depend on the harmony of their parts—he mentioned sunlight, the gleam of lightning, and the luster of stars in the sky—and this enabled him to claim, like Plato, that there are absolute forms of beauty existing in their own right. According to Plotinus, the beauty of color exists in unity derived from form, and because color overcomes the darkness lying deep within matter through the participation of light—and light, as he thought, is both logos and idea. That is why fire, in comparison to other bodies, remains beautiful. Since fire lacks its own bodily substance, it rises above other substances and approaches the immaterial. Moreover, Plotinus claims that since fire provides warmth to other bodies and maintains its own heat, it is immediately colored by color, whereas other bodies take the idea of color from fire itself. Plotinus concludes that fire radiates light and glows with light as if it were the very idea itself; meanwhile, those substances that remain out of reach of fire cannot be called beautiful, because they are vague and devoid of beauty.[7] He also notes that color comes into being when a shining substance encounters matter, and vanishes when the surface of some body ceases to have relations to light.[8] Despite various interpretations of how color comes into being and manifests itself, the very fact that ancient Greek thinkers contemplated the subject reveals a great deal about the importance of color as a visual phenomenon.

However, an author who belongs to late antiquity—the Roman architectural theorist Vitruvius—was hardly interested in metaphysical explanations of color's nature or essence; he was much more captivated by the practical application of color in architecture. In his treatise on architecture *De architectura Libri Decem*, Vitruvius classified colors into those that are natural and those that are created artificially. He scru-

---

7. Plotinus, *The Six Enneads*, 22.
8. Ibid., 188.

pulously explained where natural materials fit for practical applications can be found, gave special attention to the issues concerning how paint might be extracted, and gave numerous practical recommendations for its application. For example, he seriously considered the question of how paint can be protected from the devastating effects of the sun's rays. Here is one of Vitruvius's typical recommendations: a master who wishes to save the color of cinnabar should, after he putties the wall and waits until the paint dries, apply a mixture of wax and oil with the help of a brush. After he completes this procedure, he must take another step: using a hot iron, he has to work hard over the whole surface, and finally the whole area has to be rubbed with a wax candle and a piece of clean linen in the same manner as sculptors work on marble statues.[9] In addition, he drew his readers' attention to the fact that materials out of which specific colors are to be extracted can not be found anywhere, but only in certain areas, which were carefully indicated in the treatise. Vitruvius' exhaustive comments about the production of artificial colors and hues points to the high technological level the application of color in Roman architecture had achieved in that period.

Although Vitruvius was not concerned with metaphysical explanations, one can find them in other Roman sources. In the second century A.D., the color black was considered the color of the earthly world; red was interpreted as having close associations with blood and fire; the golden hue (a substitute for yellow) bore association with people who have left this world for a better one; and white with an eon in which those chosen by God will live after their human existence is completed. In the sixth century, another Roman, Cassiodorus, treated colors as having direct links to the seasons: green was related to spring, blue—to winter, red—to summer, and white—to autumn.[10]

EXPLANATIONS OF COLOR IN THE MIDDLE AGES AND THE RENAISSANCE

The strong need for symbolism awakened by early Christianity had a powerful response in the religious-philosophical imagination of the period, so it is no wonder that colors came to be associated with metaphysical categories. However, at the beginning, treatises where the sym-

---

9. Vitruvius, *Ten Books on Architecture*, 217.
10. Ladner, *God, Cosmos, and Humankind*, 116.

bolism of colors were justified and explained were scarce. It was only about a thousand years after Christianity came into being that these numbers grew considerably. These treatises, as a rule, discussed a defined number of colors—from seven to twelve. The greatest religious thinkers of the twelfth century—Honorius of Autun, Hugh of St. Victor, Jean d'Avranche, and others—attempted to explain color on numerous occasions. Their opinions on the meaning of the three basic colors were almost the same: white was considered as the one that expresses chastity and innocence; black —abstention and torment; and red —passion, martyrdom, and sacrifice. Abbot Suger, when creating his iconographical program and design of St. Denis, had an adequate understanding not only of light, but also of the spiritual meaning of colors and how they could serve to enhance the religious mood of those attending the mass. Meanwhile, his fierce life-long opponent St. Bernard of Clairvaux, who sought asceticism and simplicity in church architecture, refused to acknowledge the role performed by color. To him it was just an external integument, a mask covering the real truths and distancing a human being from them; accordingly, colors, like all other vanities of this earthly life, were thought to have no place in a Christian sanctuary.

The medieval understanding in its explanation of colors might seem somewhat superficial and simplistic. For example, St. Thomas Aquinas, one of the greatest spiritual authorities of the period, claimed that there are three conditions for beauty: firstly, purity or perfection; secondly, conformity or suitability; and thirdly, clarity, because as he maintains, things that have a bright color are considered beautiful.[11] Could one have a more elementary and utterly simple notion of beauty? How could this great mind, who laid the foundations for the philosophical scholasticism of the Middle Ages, give such an elementary explanation for a complex and complicated problem? However, the simplicity of this reasoning about colors could only surprise those who have no knowledge of the spirit of medieval culture, which encompasses a very close relationship between experienced reality and its comprehension. One should bear in mind that while considering the medieval theoretical conception of color, we must take into account the pervasive role of everyday reality, which had a profound impact on the thinkers of this period. The authors who interpreted phenomena related to color in a somewhat naïve and simplistic way—at least as it seems to our present "scientific" reasoning—

---

11. Aquinas, *The Summa Theologica*, 211.

were imbued with a spontaneous and whole-hearted feeling for distinct, bright, pure colors. This troubled and dramatic period of human history, marked by such common natural disasters as plague and fires as well as devastating wars, produced a special kind of imagination, thus it is not surprising that people of this epoch had an exalted fascination for everything that was colorful, lustrous, shining, glittering, and immediately captured the eye of an onlooker ready to embrace the momentous visual beauty of the world. This was a feeling for everything beautiful, for anything that agitated the emotions and the mind. Medieval people were captured by the luster of metal and gold, by fine, colorful clothing, flags waving in the wind, and in fact everything smart, luxurious, and splendid. Their aesthetic evaluations and judgement of things and phenomena, as one can judge from the literary accounts of the period, had a peculiar, almost child-like sincerity and naïve simplicity. According to Umberto Eco, it is only if one ignores their deeply imbedded feeling for color that such statements—like the one made by St. Thomas Aquinas, claiming that only brightly colored objects can be considered beautiful—could seem naïve and banal to us. It is just the opposite—this is the case where the mind of a thinker is strongly affected by the common outlook dominating during a specific historical period.[12]

Dutch cultural historian Johannes Huizinga, who thoroughly discussed the relationship between the everyday experience of beauty and its theoretical reflection in his seminal book *The Waning of the Middle Ages*, has shown the enormous impact the phenomena of visible beauty produced on medieval people. Among numerous writings in which the eyewitnesses of this epoch expressed their fascination with the luster, shining, and twinkling of beautiful pure colors, he mentions a treatise called *Blason de couleurs*, written by Herold Sicilia, which devotes an entire chapter to describing his fascination with colors. In Huizinga's view, this rather naïve piece of writing reflects an intuitive feeling for bright and pure colors typical for medieval dwellers. The author of the treatise expresses his preference for the color red—the most beautiful of all—as well as contempt for brown—the ugliest of colors. However, Huizinga notes, he especially admires the color green, and among the best combinations of colors he mentions those of light yellow and pale blue, orange and white, orange and rose, rose and white, and black and white, among several others. The combination of pale blue and green,

---

12. Eco, *Art and Beauty in the Middle Ages*, 4–17.

as well as green and red, are quite common, but he refuses to recognize them as beautiful. The insightful cultural historian notes the limited vocabulary used for describing colors: Sicilia writes about a number of hues using very simple descriptions.[13] These very medieval reflections on color represent a simplified, poorly conceptualized feeling for color that is, however, very true to its epoch, and one that can hardly be found in other forthcoming historical periods. Semi-philosophical reflections on visible sights only transfers to the field of theoretical considerations the things most dear to the eyes of medieval contemporaries, the things that enlarge the sensitivity of a common man to the beauty of nature and the environment, the feeling for bright and pure colors, for limpid daylight. The hypnotism of pure, clear colors and transparent light were perhaps best expressed in the stained glass of gothic cathedrals, where a spontaneous, instantaneous feeling for colors was transformed into another quality—the manifestation of absolute spirituality overcoming the human senses and mind. Pure colors dominate in medieval painting as well. Their uses in a picture were strictly regulated by Christian traditions and canons established by the Church, which was the highest authority and arbiter throughout the Middle Ages. According to the medieval concept of nature, mixing, splitting, or joining elements was considered the work of the Devil, and interrupted the order established by the Creator. This explains why pure colors dominate not only in art, but in other spheres of medieval culture as well, though as time passed and social organization and hierarchy became more complex, the range of colors became significantly wider. This method of using color, which dominated in western European art up to the fifteenth century, is called heraldic by the English art historian and philosopher Herbert Read, who emphasized that these limits of range were not necessarily a drawback, as one can judge from the "beauty, balance and clarity" of medieval painting.[14]

During the Renaissance, the Aristotelian interpretation of colors resurfaced. Italian architect and architectural theorist Leon Battista Alberti, following Aristotle, contended that the nature of the color red is related to fire; that of blue or blue-gray—to air; green—to water; while the earth was identified with the color of ashes. According to Alberti, black and white are not true colors exactly; they are instead the modulators of colors. He also noted the importance to human sight of the links

13. Huizinga, *Viduramžių ruduo*, 343.
14. Read, *The Meaning of Art*, 44.

between colors and light, pointing out that the scale of these links can realized when observing the falling of darkness: whenever light disappears, colors vanish, and when light comes into being once again—it brings back colors in their full strength.[15] In his treatise on architecture, another distinguished Renaissance architectural theorist, Antonio Filarete, in addressing his patron, the duke of Milano, argued for the existence of six basic colors: black, white, red, yellow, blue, and green. Each of these colors, except black and white, has its equivalent in nature: the red one is equal to fire, blue—to the sky, green—to grass, yellow—to flowers. He claimed that there are three colors that can be combined without fear, and these are yellow, red, and green.

Contemplation of color was by no means the exclusive province of architects. One of the greatest Renaissance minds, Leonardo da Vinci, provided his own insights into the nature of colors. Contradicting philosophers, most of whom claimed that neither white nor black are colors, Leonardo insisted that among simple colors, white is the primary color because it is provided by light, while yellow represents the earth, green represents water, blue stands for air, and red for darkness. He associated the color black with total darkness (or absence of light), and conceived of it as standing above the element of fire, because there is neither a substance, nor a dimension where the rays of sun could encounter it. However, one should beware of direct parallels between the thinking of Leonardo and Aristotle. It is generally thought that Leonardo came across Aristotle's treatise *De coloribus* around the year 1506, but appropriated only a part of the thinker's concepts —he borrowed only those elements of it that suited his own understanding of color. Contradicting the authority of Aristotle, Leonardo refused to admit that blue and green are simple colors: in his opinion blue, like air, is made out of light and darkness (black being the most dark, and white the most transparent); meanwhile, green was made from blue and yellow.[16]

And yet the architects were the ones who maintained a constant interest in theoretical musings on color. Italian architect Andrea Palladio—a thoughtful and pragmatic master of the High Renaissance period—gave his own views on the use of color in the decoration of buildings. In his second book on architecture, while discussing the forms of sanctuaries and requirements for their construction, Palladio

15. Alberti, *On Painting and Sculpture*, 45.
16. Kemp, *The Science of Art*, 268.

wrote that there is no other color more suitable for the purpose of decorating Christian sanctuaries than white. He considered white exceptional because its brightness is especially favored by God. Whenever a sanctuary is painted in white, it does not allow other colors to lead the human soul away from the contemplation of heavenly things; moreover, it forces humans to maintain a rigidness of mind, and to be close to things that pour light on their souls, putting them into the service of the Creator and good works.[17]

However, one should be aware that this line of thought was conditioned not only by the traditional symbolism of colors, but also by another, more earthly factor: during this period there was a widespread but erroneous opinion that held that the decoration of the buildings of antiquity was predominately monochromatic. Renaissance town dwellers inherited neglected, corroded, faded, rain-washed Roman ruins, and they assumed they had always appeared that way. They were not aware that the flow of time had devastated the polychromic decorations of ancients buildings as well as their smaller decorative details, and only the strongest and most monumental architectural structures had survived in, as a rule, deteriorated condition. They firmly believed that neither Romans nor Greeks (and the architectural legacy of the latter was unknown to Europeans during the Renaissance) used any colors to decorate their buildings. This opinion was eventually abandoned, but it took centuries for new evidence to surface. The architectural theorists of the nineteenth century, who had a much better knowledge based on polychromic research, no longer shared the belief that the architecture of antiquity was monochromic. In 1834, the German architectural theorist Gottfried Semper, basing his opinion on data provided by the findings made during the excavations at Pompeii, concluded that the old masters knew how to use "remarkably pure colors," thus he considered the discussion about whether Romans had used a polychromic system to be already exhausted.[18] The importance of bright colors in the decoration of North European cathedrals of the late Middle Ages was emphasized by the British art historian and critic John Ruskin, who insisted that he did not know of a single monument belonging to any serious architectural school that did not contain a coating of paint, mosaic, or gold.[19] The role

17. Palladio, *The Four Books on Architecture*, II.
18. Semper, *The Four Elements*, 59–60.
19. Ruskin, *The Lamp of Beauty*, 226.

of colors in medieval architecture is particularly emphasized by Abbot Suger in his diary, where he says that the first thing the masters he commissioned from different regions had to do was to fix fractures in the old walls and cover them with "gold and precious materials."[20]

THE DEVELOPMENT OF COLOR CONCEPTS SINCE THE ENLIGHTENMENT

The sensual attitude toward the understanding of color once set forth by Plato in *Philebus* was revitalized during the advent of modern times in the philosophical reasoning of the Enlightenment, although devoid of metaphysical speculations. Immanuel Kant claimed that

> A mere color, for instance the green of a lawn, and a mere tone ... are by most people called beautiful in themselves, though both seem to depend upon mere matter [as opposed to form] of our ideas, namely simple sensations, and so only deserve the name of pleasant or charming. We may, however, note here that the sensation of colour and tone have the claim to be counted beautiful, so far, but so far only, as they are *pure*. For purity is a character of their form and also the only character of these ideas which can certainly be universally appreciated.[21]

This statement revivifying Plato's dictum, instead of explaining the problem of understanding color, makes it more clumsy. This ambiguity of Kant's statement was taken note of by the British neo-Hegelian philosopher Bernard Bosanquet, who justly remarked that this explanation, "which reminds us of Plato, would not bear interpretation either by physical analysis or by direct perception. The eye and ear do not necessarily tell us which colours and sounds have the most uniform physical causes; nor, if either sense or science detects a mixture of tones or spectrum of colours, do we necessarily judge that mixture to be devoid of aesthetic purity, much less of aesthetic beauty."[22]

This insightful remark of Kant's critic urges a revisitation of that period of modern era during which the problem of color was transferred from the dimension of metaphysical musings to the sphere of a new one—scientific analysis. Cambridge Neoplatonist bishop George

---

20. Suger, *On the Abbey Church*, 43.
21. Carrit, *Philosophies of Beauty*, 115.
22. Bosanquet, *A History of Aesthetics*, 268.

Berkeley, in his seminal treatise *New Theory of Vision*, claimed that the sense of color is caused by irritation of the eye's retina. Later, in the second half of the nineteenth century, when the need for seemingly objective knowledge based on empirical data became more prominent, relations between the interests of art and science became increasingly intimate. The spirit of positivism that was taking a strong hold on Western culture gave a powerful impetus to artists, urging them not only to observe and depict nature, but to interpret reality scientifically, and to base their intuitive insights and findings on data provided by the natural sciences. Of course, the great British painter Joseph William Mallord Turner had already expanded the notion of the relationship between light and color in his canvases somewhat earlier, paving the way to future experiments and the findings of Paris' impressionists. And despite the indignation of Turner's conservative contemporaries, the prospects of this tendency were appreciated by such an authority on the artistic expression of his day as John Ruskin, who gave a comprehensive account of his views on color and its role in architecture in his famous Oxford lectures. Ruskin maintained that only form could be absolute; color, on the other hand, was relative, and this fact was proved by the discontinuity of color relations in space. In his book *The Stones of Venice*, Ruskin wrote:

> And when we use abstract colours, we are in fact using a part of nature herself, —using a quality of her light, correspondent with that of the air, to carry sound; and the arrangement of colour in harmonious masses is again a matter of treatment, not selection. Yet even in this separate art of colouring, as referred to architecture, it is very notable that the best tints are always of natural stones. These can hardly be wrong; I think I never yet saw an offensive introduction of the natural colours of marble and precious stone, unless in small mosaics, and in one or two glaring instances of the resolute determination to produce something ugly at any cost.[23]

Among other things, he drew attention to the special way of rendering the relationship between color and lighting practiced in the fifteenth century by the Venice school of painting. According to Ruskin, representatives of this school realized far better than anyone else that when colors are submerged in shadow they become darker, however, they do not become pale, and often get more expressive: the beauty of the

---

23. Ruskin, *The Stones of Venice*, 221.

blue and purple colors of nature is most visible in mountains covered by shadow in the background of an amber sky.[24] He also asserted that abstract color is not an imitation of nature—it is nature itself; thus the pleasure provided by the color blue or red is the same in all cases if the splendor of a hue is homogeneous, no matter whether it is produced by a human being, or opens in a flower, or is created by the chemistry of the sky. Shortly afterwards, the impressionists, rebelling against the stale canons of their epoch, adopted the same method of studying the relationship between color and light that was mapped by the pioneering experiments of their forerunner, "illustrious Turner." The passionate strife for new methods of painting and a totally new style went hand in hand with the rapid and almost revolutionary shifts in scientific research of natural phenomena. The theory of splitting light into composite colors and their harmonization, introduced by Michel Eugène Chevreul, was adopted as a tool for artist's work by many Parisian painters of that time by using what one might call scientifically-based artistic experiments. The effort to support methods of painting by applying the results of scientific research are illustrated by a remark of George Seurat, who posed a question to himself: if he was able to discover scientific laws of color in his practical work, why could he not find a scientific system of painting endowed with the same logic, enabling the artist to tune lines in the same way he tunes colors?[25]

One should not forget that the theoretical analysis of color could already have been based on science instead of just metaphysical musings, considering the research done by such scientists as Rene Descartes, Robert Boyle, Isaac Newton, and Newton's ardent opponent Johann Wolfgang Goethe—poet, scholar and natural scientist almost equal in his range of interests to the great Renaissance figures, and the author of *Theory of Colors*—as well as the treatises of other perhaps less important individuals. Rene Descartes rejected a misleading presumption claiming that colors are mixtures of light and shadow. Descartes argued that all space is filled with ether, and that light makes its way through a thick mass of invisible particles. English physicist and chemist Robert Boyle agreed with his predecessor, and rejected the theory of the origin of colors based on the relationship between white and black: instead he claimed that all hues are to be found in white light. One could suggest

---

24. Ruskin, *Lectures on Art*, 220.
25. Read, *A Concise History*, 28.

that the most essential, almost revolutionary advancement was made in the second half of the seventeenth century when Isaac Newton began his experiments in the sphere of optics. It is Newton who is credited with discovering the structure of the color wheel. With the help of special optical devices, including prisms, he carried out experiments in 1666 that proved the entire spectrum of colors exists in white light. However, one should take into consideration that the system he devised to organize color was not merely based on a positivist analysis: his classification of the seven colors—red, orange, yellow, green, blue, indigo, and violet—corresponded to the seven diatonic notes in music and the seven heavenly spheres discussed by the Pythagoreans. Not every Newtonian assumption proved to be precise, and as soon as the Dutch scientist Christian Huygens carried out his research, Newton was forced to make corrections to some of his premature conclusions. But because of his sophisticated system of speculations and experiments, readers and even critics of Newton failed to understand the problem, and there was far less discussion than there could have been. And it seemed that Newton had researched every possible physical aspect of color, ranging from the ultimate causes of feeling for color to the details of specific mixtures of pigment. It was only discovered much later that not only Newton's, but Maxwell's and Chevreul's theories were grounded on the misleading assumption that claimed all colors can be produced by mixing pigments of three colors with white and black. Like the scientists who preceded him and those who came after him, Newton was ready to search for analogous principles in the structure of sound and music. He guessed that rays of light move through mediators periodically, in the same way that vibrations in air, depending on their size, produce experiences of several sounds. This agreed with an argument of Descartes, who claimed that color is a sense of the eye produced by mechanical action, but not a quality of the object itself. According to renowned Oxford scholar Martin Kemp, who has published brilliant research on the historical relations between art and science, this analogy was provided with mathematically precise reasoning, and one can claim that Newton's effort to create a mathematical-musical system of colors determined the development of his ideas.[26] Johann Wolfgang Goethe, who published a study in 1810 based on his own experiments regarding physical stimuli and perception, was deeply affected by alchemical concepts of color, which,

---

26. Kemp, *The Science of Art*, 286.

in their own way, were influenced by the ideas of the Gnostics. He had a reserved and skeptical view of Newton's "mystical" number of seven colors, and was instead influenced by German mystic thinker Jacob Boehme, who claimed that the single color—white—reflects divinity rather than a secret of nature. According to Goethe, there are two basic colors—yellow and blue. These colors have a special quality: when they are mixed, a third color—green—comes into being.[27] Goethe concluded that all colors originated from a mixture of light and darkness, and their theory, together with the phenomenon of optics, is a manifestation of universal polarity, which can be perceived with the help of the theory of magnetism, electricity, and chemistry. He wrote that "Colors are acts of light; their modification is active and passive," and this can help to explain light itself. The relation between colors and light is especially intimate; however both colors and light as a whole belong to nature, because nature opens itself to sight through these two in a special way.[28] Goethe attempted to relate the qualities of colors experienced by human senses to ethical categories. The four spiritual peculiarities of a human being were related to the six colors of a circle he drew: warm colors were attached to reason and education, cold colors—to sensuality and imagination. The color yellow was interpreted as the one closest to light, since it is bright, noble, and creates an impression of warmth; the color blue is close to darkness, as it is cold, gloomy, and melancholic; red expresses gravity, dignity, charm; green—pleasure and convenience.[29] He identified the color yellow with reason, blue with understanding, green with sensuality, and purple with imagination. According to Goethe, colors can be used allegorically, symbolically, and mystically. He also strongly emphasized the relationship between color and sound. Although they can not be directly compared, color and sound refer to a universal formula, and both are derivative. Using a poetic metaphor, Goethe spoke of color and sound as two rivers that spring from the same source but take different ways in different regions and never collide. Arguing against Newton, Goethe attempted to revive Aristotelian theory; however, despite his deep insights into the physiological and psychological effects of colors, he was wrong to put together such different phenomena as energy, the speed of light waves, their frequency, and visual perception.

27. Goethe, *Goethe's Color Theory*, 20.
28. Ibid., 71.
29. Ibid., 168–74.

In this sense, his theory was surpassed by his contemporary and fellow countryman—the German Romanticist painter Phillip Otto Runge, who published his treatise titled *Farbenkuler* the same year as Goethe.

The nineteenth century was marked with an abundance of research into color. The English physicists Thomas Young published an important volume on the structure of color in 1802; somewhat later, in 1832, the treatise of J. C. Le Blon was published. Le Blon argued that red, yellow, and blue have to be treated as primary colors. Meanwhile, in the beginning of the century, the renowned Scottish physicist James Clark Maxwell published works that were of utmost importance. The theory of three primary colors, which was supported by Le Blon, Goethe, Chevreul, and other scientists, is usually associated with the name of Sir David Brewster, who wrote a treatise on optics and is considered one of its main founders. These scientists were joined by artists, whose minds throughout the nineteenth century were captivated by the idea that findings made with the help of aesthetic experience and intuition could be transformed into what was thought to be the laws of objective understanding of reality. The age of science seemed to promise the possibility of solving each and every mystery of nature and humankind; it looked like experimental science would present a key to all the secrets of the universe—a belief that was shared by many artists of that period. It is hardly surprising that the Renaissance idea of establishing bridges between the arts and science was reborn in a milieu of visual artists, and among painters especially. Wassily Kandinsky, an expatriate artist from Russia who settled in Western Europe and was absorbed by the findings of physics and optics, set out to devise a highly original theory of colors based on artistic experiments, science, and philosophical reasoning, which, as he hoped, would explain the role of color in painting and its effect on human perception. Kandinsky stressed the importance of the physical and psychic effects of color, and he argued that by using combinations of color in a harmonious way the artist is capable "of touching the human soul."[30] His short but ambitious treatise *On Spirituality in Art* was an attempt to demonstrate the close relationship between visual arts and music, and to draw parallels between these distinct arts. According to Kandinsky, the relationship between form and color allows us to realize the importance of form to color; meanwhile color contains its own "inner sounding" and has a spiritual presence. He also made an attempt

---

30. Kandinsky, *O dukovnom*, 44.

to explain the qualities of colors and their effect on vision and the moods of a human being. And yet, it is important to note that in his theory, the effect of color was not identified with the usual emotions. For example, while discussing the peculiarities of blue, Kandinsky notes that when it becomes darker, it becomes deeper, and creates a feeling of infinity; it triggers a wish to know what is beyond sensuality, and this should be related to spirituality or religiosity instead of the human senses. Blue was described as a "typically heavenly" color, the depth of which contains an element of peace.[31] Green was associated with silence and stillness: it was the most tranquil color. He treated green as neutral, in the sense that it does not cause either joy or pain or passion. Whether brighter or darker, green produces an effect of indifference or peace. Meanwhile, the tones of yellow disseminate spiritual warmth on the canvas of a painting. White, according to the artist, presents itself as a symbol of a universe in which everything has disappeared: colors and material qualities as well as substances.[32] That is why the color white represents a soundless and voiceless world, and when this world acquires material shape, it appears unreachable, distant, and as if it were stretching toward infinity. Kandinsky suggests that the inner sounding of white can be based on a musical analogy: sounds are like pauses that interrupt the main theme for a short period, but never become the end of the work's action: it sounds like a silence that could be understood. Accordingly, Kandinsky equates the sounding of the color black to Nothingness, but a kind of Nothingness that is dominated by a silence that gives no hope at all.[33] Insisting that certain combination of colors inevitably provoke certain feelings and moods as well as breakthroughs of emotions and spirituality, the artist was constructing a theory which, despite the fact that it was grounded on scientific data available at the time, was totally alien to positivist interpretations of reality; as such it was much closer to metaphysical and mystical doctrines, since Kandinsky attempted to go beyond anything that could be classified as pure experimental science. The analogies between color and musical harmony were of special interest to other modernist painters, especially abstractionists. Mikalojus Konstantinas Čiurlionis, regarded as the most outstanding and original Lithuanian painter, explored them in his painting independent of

31. Ibid., 69.
32. Ibid., 72.
33. Ibid., 73.

Kandinsky, though he left no theoretical reflections on these problems. One can also recall the French painter Nicolas Poussin, who compared the peculiarities of expression of forms and colors with ancient musical tones long before western modernism came into being.

Fernand Leger, who was particularly interested in the psychological effect of colors and far less, if at all, concerned about their metaphysical aspects, emphasized the close links between colors and human emotions. He claimed that pure colors should be "alive" both internally and externally, so that their values could be brought to a maximum; thus a square meter of yellow dominates a surface four times larger; meanwhile, any piece of furniture in red is capable of dominating in a large space over pieces decorated in any other hues.[34] Leger's insights went beyond the role of color in painting: he justly argued that colors help to create the image and character of any closed space. For example, he emphasized that colors have the power to change spatial perception: a room painted in a bright blue color creates the effect of moving a wall further back, so the space looks larger than it is; meanwhile, when the same room is painted in black, the wall optically comes closer to the beholder; and when the wall is painted all over in yellow—it simply disappears. However, when these three colors are brought together in dynamic contrast, the wall might be optically destroyed.[35] These important insights into the capacity of color to affect spatial relations stimulated other modernist artists to experiment with colors; however, the psychology of visual art eventually provided a better and more systematic understanding of how the human mind perceives different colors, hues, and their combinations.

Somewhat later an émigré from Germany to United States, art historian and architectural theorist Rudolf Arnheim, focused his research on the problems of art perception, and provided a detailed account of the psychological effect of colors on human vision. Among other things, he corroborated the insights of the French artist Fernand Leger mentioned earlier. Summarizing the data of his optical experiments, Arnheim gave a thorough description of how colors and their hues are perceived by a human being, analyzed combinations of different colors in a work of art (mostly painting), and discussed principles and conformities with the laws of color harmony. Among his many pioneering findings was the

34. Clarke, *Architectural Stained Glass*, 20.
35. Leger, "On Monumentality," 42.

conclusion that categories such as "cold" or "warm" say little when one attempts to describe pure hues, and that the stronger effect on perception is made not by a primary hue, but by the one which deviates from it slightly. This law states that the influence on perception is stronger not in those cases when two colors of equal value are mixed, but in those where the environment of color elucidates either the assimilation of colors or their contrasts. Pure primary colors, such as red, yellow or blue, look neither dynamic nor expressive. The peculiarities of expression become more visible when color, because of its tendency to become another color, creates an effect of dynamics. But the expressiveness and "temperature" of color is created not only by a hue, but by other factors: distinctness and richness.[36] These factors all influence the harmony of colors, but harmony is essential only in the respect that all colors of a composition must correspond to the common whole. Basing his considerations of color harmony on musical analogy, Arnheim claimed that traditional versions of this kind of theory are far less universal than their founders initially thought them. A curious example of such universalist pretensions is Ostwald's law, formulated in 1919, which claimed that rich colors should be used in small quantities, as a large space of a color like red looks rough. However, Arnheim goes on, this law becomes arguable whenever one thinks of the famous picture of Henri Matisse, which occupies four square meters, all painted in a distinct red. This example allowed him to conclude that anything presented as an absolute norm is nothing more than the expression of a fashion that reigned in that particular period.[37] On the other hand, the color wheel modeled by Ostwald was much less concerned with the essence of light or paint than with the powers of vision.

The English art historian Herbert Read provided a useful classification of colors' role in the visual arts. He distinguished among four ways of using color in a work of art: first, heraldic; second, natural; third, harmonious; and fourth, pure. According to Read, when colors are used naturally, their goal is to provide a diversified variety by adding to the other plastic elements of a work of art—line, tone, etc. When a color is used for symbolic reasons, it can be described as a heraldic model (as in children's drawings or medieval paintings). A color is used harmoniously when an artist, taking into consideration the play of light and

36. Arnheim, *Art and Visual Perception*, 331–71.
37. Ibid., 349.

shade, adjusts colors to the dominating tone of the picture. Read related a pure way of using color to the discovery of Cezanne, who found that a color can reveal form without depending on the shifts in light and shade, and that in such cases the most intense colors are used and the spatial effect is created by a tonal gradation of colors.[38]

A different approach toward understanding and explaining the essence of color was taken by George Santayana, who in his *Sense of Beauty* provided a sensualistic account of color, drawing parallels between color and form. According to Santayana,

> Form, which is almost synonymous of beauty, is for us usually something visible: it is a synthesis of the seen. But prior to the effect of form, which arises in the constructive imagination, comes the effect of color; this is purely sensuous, and no better intrinsically than the effects of any other sense; but being more involved in the perception of objects than are the rest, it becomes more readily an element of beauty."[39]

THE SYMBOLISM OF COLOR

Color is closely and intrinsically related to symbol. Though the origin of symbols and their relationship to objects of a particular meaning is far from being clear, and is explained differently in many theories that aspire to an explanatory role, there is no doubt that symbol and color have natural bonds of meaning. Steen Eiler Rasmussen, a distinguished Danish architect and architectural theorist, has noted that color is used symbolically in many ways: there are special colors to forward a message or warning; there are national and regional colors; there are colors that are used by different schools, clubs, and associations. This seems to be common knowledge; however, Rasmussen goes on to say that it is rather difficult to explain why we associate certain colors to certain things. Besides, the reception of colors changes with shifts in the lighting of some objects—for example, when food loses its natural colors, people as a rule lose their taste for food. Moreover, although some colors produce almost the same universal psychological effects (like red or green, which are associated with passion and peace respectively), most color

---

38. Read, *The Meaning of Art*, 42–44.
39. Santayana, "A Sense of Beauty," 199.

conventions depend upon the particular civilization.[40] The symbolism of color was deeply rooted in ancient cultures, and each had its own esoteric tradition. Symbolical colors are used to this very day in the sand painting of Navajo Indians in the southwest of North America; meanwhile, in the so-called western vernacular culture, black is usually associated with death and decay, white with serenity and purity, and red with rage.[41] The most important buildings of ancient civilizations—oriented as a rule according to the arrangement of cosmic bodies in the sky—were decorated in colors that contained and conveyed certain meanings. Among both civilized and primitive cultures, colors perform the role of a common language that conveys metaphysical, philosophical, and religious doctrines. This language is shared among members of particular communities within a particular culture itself. The ancient city of Ectabana—as we can judge from the descriptions of an eyewitness, the historian Herodotus—was protected by seven walls, and each ring of the wall was painted according to the colors of the seven planets described by Persian magicians. Or, say, another ancient monument—the ziggurat, the astronomic Babylonian tower of God—was also divided into seven parts, rising from its base up to the sky, and each segment was painted in a different color corresponding to each of the seven planets. The Lithuanian architectural historian Rimantas Buivydas notes that according to Zoroastrian interpretation of the sacred model of Vara, the different colors of the four entrance gates had a specific symbolical meaning: blue symbolized wisdom, steadiness, and glory; white—concord, accomplishment, and truth; red—goodness, will, and activity; and green—reason, intellect, and eternity.[42] The Spanish art historian and Jesuit scholar Juan Edouard Cirlot, who wrote one of the best dictionaries of symbology, provided the most universal interpretation of the symbolic meanings of colors: blue, related to Jupiter and Juno, gods of the heavens, stands for religious feeling, devotedness, and serenity; green, related to Venus and Nature, expresses fertility, compassion, and adjustments; violet signifies nostalgia and memories because it originates from blue (devotedness) and red (passion); yellow, the color of Apollo, the god of the sun, symbolizes magnanimity, intuition, and reason; orange signifies dignity and ambition; red, being the attribute

---

40. Rasmussen, *Experiencing Architecture*, 218.
41. Williamson and Cummins, *Light and Color*, 4.
42. Buivydas, "Simbolis ir architektūra," 93.

of Mars, means passion, sensuality, and vitality; and gray expresses neutrality, egoism, depression, inertia, and indifference, meanings that originate from the color of ashes.[43] However, the meanings of colors thus indicated are of a synthetic character, and one should not forget that in each culture and every particular epoch color or its hues had a more strictly demarcated meaning. For example, Marija Gimbutas, the Lithuania-American ethno-archeologist, professor at Harvard and California universities and a media celebrity of her time, emphasized that the colors black and white meant completely different things in Old European and Indo-European cultures. The inhabitants of Old Europe (before Indo-Europeans settled in the area) associated black with fertility and mother Earth, but among Indo-Europeans black symbolized the god of death. White was perceived as the color of bones, which symbolized death for the Old Europeans, while for Indo-Europeans it was the color of God and heaven.[44] But even if these observations about the variety of the symbolism of colors in different civilizations and colors in some particular contexts is true, it is equally difficult to argue that the symbolism of colors in different cultures is controversial. Poet and philosopher Fredrick Turner has drawn our attention to the research done by his father, the renowned anthropologist Victor Turner, regarding parallels between the color symbolism of Central Africa's religious and body painting and its European and American counterparts. Red in all these cultures meant bloodshed, menstruation, and life; white—milk, sperm, and unearthly brightness; black—evil, impurity, death, and the mystical darkness of appearance.[45]

It is well known that symbols are of utmost importance to different religious systems, state powers, and communities alike. The ancient cultures were famous for institutionalizing the usage and purpose of specific colors. For example, in ancient Beijing, the color white was exclusively reserved for the decoration of the emperor's palace, and no person of any other rank could use it for painting his own dwelling. In ancient Chinese and Japanese cultures, yellow was the privilege of the emperor. Even later, in medieval European culture, canons of art established which particular color could (and should) be used for representing one or another biblical character to make him easily identifiable by

43. Cirlot, *A Dictionary of Symbols*, 52–53.
44. Gimbutienė, *Senoji Europa*, 292.
45. Turner, *Beauty*, 97.

even the least educated individual. For example, a combination of blue and purple was canonical for representing the Virgin Mary. True, it took some time until such canons were finally established: up until the twelfth century the robe of the Virgin Mary was painted in dark colors (black, gray, brown, violet, or dark green), because the artists who painted these images attempted to stress her grief and mourning over the crucifixion and eventual death of Jesus. However, in the course of the twelfth century the color blue began to dominate, and at the end of century, because of the influence of so-called "chromofiles," it became brighter.[46]

The interpretations of symbols that emerged in modern times, influenced and shaped by the powerful and long-lasting theories of Sigmund Freud and Carl Gustav Jung, as well as semiotical interpretations, often prevent us adequately comprehending the authentic meanings of symbols in earlier epochs, when psychoanalytical attitudes were not yet born. Contemporary notions of symbols, grounded in psychology, paradoxically make the dimension of symbolism far more narrow: symbols these days are "read" not through the eyes of men and women who lived in the surrounding ocean of symbols and took them to be as natural as any other earthly realities, but through the eyes of individuals who are educated as skeptics and whose minds are affected by the so-called scientific worldview. Despite the fundamental changes in human perception, one should not forget that even in contemporary culture (especially in those dimensions related to the religious sphere) the usage of colors continues to be based on old traditions, even though their origins are not always known. This should be taken into consideration in architecture, especially by those architects working for various religious communities. Contemporary church buildings in different parts of the world occasionally show signs that the links between traditional symbolism and colors have regretfully been lost. This is especially true of those societies that, for various reasons, experienced a break in the history of their religious life, like many eastern European countries during the reign of Communism, when religious belief was considered an enemy of the state's power and ruling ideology. A dozen or so of the Catholic churches built during a couple of recent decades in my own country, Lithuania, indicate that establishing bonds between religious traditions, colors, and architectural practice remains a problem for a number of architects who matured in the climate of the laic (or perhaps

---

46. Pastoreau, *Blue: The History of a Color*, 50.

openly atheist) culture that dominated eastern Europe for almost half of the last century.

The processes of secularization triggered by a consciousness shaped during Renaissance and eventually accelerated by the European Enlightenment resulted in a decline of interest in the rich dimensions of symbolism. These essential changes in the consciousness of a secularized human being were addressed in the study *Art as Symbol*, written by the theologian Rainer Volp, in which he proves that white—liturgically the most meaningful color—can no longer be regarded as only a symbol of belief or worship in contemporary art.[47] On the other hand, despite the process of secularization and the scientifically-minded atheist worldview shaped by the modern epoch, imprints of decaying or vanished symbolic meanings continue to exist in the collective consciousness, together with many other contradictory elements. Thus, no matter the individual preferences, attitudes, or convictions, certain shapes—like that of the cross—are still associated with suffering and the Resurrection, while white and black signify the eternal opposition between light and darkness, goodness and evil, or the poles of life and death. And precisely because of this persistence of meanings rooted in the human mind, not only religious or sacred architecture, but also many other architectural structures still maintain the potential of awaking a layer of collective consciousness and imagination where symbols can surface. No matter how one interprets the semantic meanings of old and new architecture, color remains an important (though perhaps not exclusive) characteristic of visible structures, and maintains strong bonds not only with psychophysical effects, but also with a world of vanished or hidden meanings that have the power of occasional resurrection.

ARCHITECTURAL COLOR IN THE URBAN MILIEU

Every historical culture, every region, country, or its particular part, every city (except perhaps for the modern *cloned* metropolises that look almost identical wherever they are) has its own character of urban coloring—one that provides the specific and memorable atmosphere of a place, that which makes it different from other places, and a quality difficult to recreate mechanically elsewhere without destroying the integrity of the overall impression. This character depends on climate, environment,

---

47. Taine, *Meno filosofija*, 33.

available building materials, local architectural traditions, and many other less significant factors. Renowned French positivist art historian and philosopher Hippolyte Taine of the nineteenth century, who, like a true child of his epoch, firmly believed that in the near future humanities will develop methods of study no less objective than those used in botany, biology, or any other natural science, was, despite his limitations, quite right in distinguishing certain regularities governing art traditions in different regions, especially those related to architecture, choice of building and decoration materials, and, last but not least, coloring. In his celebrated two-volume book *Philosophie de'l Art*, Taine drew readers' attention to the fact that a set of factors exist that produce a strong effect on the color scheme of individual buildings and the character of a settlement or town more generally. Among a number of examples selected to prove his insights, he chose to focus on Flemish cities, claiming the specific climate and peculiarities of soil influenced the traditions associated with building materials and use of color schemes. Taine noticed that this alluvial country cannot boast of having any stone, and that is why only materials such as terra cotta, brick and tile are used for building houses. Since it often rains in the region, the roofs of the houses are sloping, and because of regular humidity the facades of the houses are covered with glaze or paint. This makes a Flemish city a network of brown, red, or brownish buildings that always look neat and clean. In this landscape one can spot an old church built from shingle or small calcified stones only on occasion. In Holland, sidewalks are made from brick with fragments of porcelain, daily cleaned with the help of water. This urban or semi-urban environment, according to Taine, is in fact responsible for the "essential character" which is reflected in climate, soil, society, and each particular individual.[48] Even if one rejects the determinism of Taine's reasoning, which was shaped by the intellectual climate of his day, and especially his belief in the rising future of science as well as moral, social, and technological progress—who has such unconditional faith in both science and progress in our century?—it is difficult to argue against his wise insights into the close links between climate, soil, building materials, and architecture, not to mention coloring.

    It is true that up to the very beginning of the nineteenth century the coloring of European cities and towns did not experience rapid changes: the shifts in urban color schemes were slow, more or less organic, and

---

48. Porter, *Architectural Color*, 37.

conditioned by local building materials and technologies, as well as by specific paints. The same can be said about architectural styles, since their evolution and changes were to a certain degree limited by the availability of building materials, and this fact influenced and disciplined the forms of buildings, which maintained close links to the human factor.[49] There are, however, exceptional cases in the history of building and architecture where colors used for decoration have virtually nothing to do with either the traditions that prevailed in that specific culture or region, nor with any attempts to harmonize color schemes. The country houses built over several centuries in certain provincial Swedish and Norwegian regions are among such curious exceptions. To this very day, many wooden houses in these Nordic countries are painted in a rich dark red or brown color, which distinguishes them from the greenery of natural surroundings in summer or the white covering of snow during winter. This unusual regularity has been an issue long debated by Nordic art historians. The opinion that has growing support lately is that this color scheme was used because Scandinavian peasants who lacked sufficient funds to build brick houses at least painted them in colors reminiscent of the burned brick used in building the local palaces and manor houses of the Swedish or Norwegian nobility.[50]

In the long run of history, the color schemes of Western European cities were never specially designed; however, the coloring of some towns became an object of planning and municipal care as far back as a couple of centuries ago. For example, it is known that Torino in Italy had a "council of builders" as early as 1800. Among the responsibilities of this municipal council was the task of creating and maintaining a color scheme for the entire city. This council survived until 1845, and although it is unknown what of this original color scheme has survived to the present, there are records indicating that it was greatly admired by visitors: at the end of the nineteenth century Friedrich Nietzsche was captured by its beauty, and somewhat later, at the beginning of the twentieth century, this color scheme of Torino impressed William James.[51]

Color, together with other architectural elements, gives a special character to a city, town, settlement, block, street, or an individual house: they become either fascinating, aesthetically impressive, monu-

49. Rasmussen, *Experiencing Architecture*, 216–17.
50. Porter, *Architectural Color*, 39–40.
51. Rasmussen, *Experiencing Architecture*, 221.

mental, or just cozy, livable, walkable, and psychologically rewarding, or, on the contrary, gloomy, depressive, repulsive, and lacking a truly human character. Some, like the author of this book, have had the experience of living in the milieu of the cold, impersonal, colorless, faceless, and senseless architecture of Soviet Communism. The destructive effects of such architecture are well known in Eastern Europe, where the Communist regime pursued identical urban and architectural policies, and it is no wonder that these days, after great social changes, post-totalitarian countries are extremely eager to overcome the mental and material legacy of a gray, colorless mass of urban architecture. It is in this area that changes in architectural aesthetic are clearly visible: former steel and concrete boxes are transformed into a lively and colorful urban mass, where sometimes harmony and common sense are abandoned in favor of immediate visible effects. This new colorful "fast-food architecture" bears strange associations with a professional orchestra that performs its musical pieces without the help of a conductor, and where each musician tries hard to strike his own note at the expense of all the others. Though one can agree with Rasmussen's observation, who notes that the use of color, like any other architectural element, is not subject to any strict rules or instructions, nevertheless a certain choice of colors for an architectural structure makes a profound impact on our aesthetic perception of an individual building or even an entire urban mass. Since there are no universally applicable formulas for applying color to architectural buildings, it is possible to conclude that in some cases success will depend on rationally calculated choice and sometimes on pure intuition. And yet, Rasmussen's insight into the role of colors in our lives is worth paying attention to: warm and cold colors express very different moods and emotions; moreover, colors change throughout the day, and even if we fail to notice their variations, our mood changes with the changes of lighting. As he rightly adds, this is especially evident in cities located close to large bodies of water, where the atmosphere is soaked with humidity.[52]

On the other hand, flaws in using color in the urban environment, together with other problems such as overcrowding, erosion of public space, and lack of greenery, result in serious social damage to communities and individuals alike. As far as our emotions are directly related to our environment, the coloring of urban architecture affects

52. Ibid., 222.

our perception and contributes to the way we feel in the urban milieu. Of course, color in architecture, compared to its other, more relevant aspects, is secondary; nevertheless, the role of color should not be overlooked. Colors can perform various functions and serve many goals, be they used for symbolic, aesthetic, or psychological reasons, such as to safeguard desired optical effects, to secure the comfort of a human being, to demarcate the function of a particular building, or to create the character of its interior spaces. However, Geoffrey Scott has drawn our attention to one more important aspect of color used in architecture. According to Scott, there undeniably is such a thing as value of space, and one of its constituent parts is color: a floor covered with dark colors and a ceiling painted in bright colors creates one sensation of a particular interior space, while the same room with a ceiling painted in dark colors and brightly colored floor will produce a totally different effect.[53] Rasmussen, who has been my guiding spirit into a proper understanding of color's role in architecture, has also observed that different optical effects in architecture can be created with the help of color alone. Comparing structures built by Le Corbusier and Mies van der Rohe, he notes that both architects were interested in creating a special optic illusion and overcoming the natural heaviness of building materials. While pursuing this goal, both architects, each in his own way, put building and decoration materials to use, but also made good use of color tones and their combinations. Designing his buildings for the town of Pessac near Bordeaux, Le Corbusier aimed to create the illusion of a weightless house. That is why he chose to paint the walls of the building in light gray and heavenly blue, and both colors encountered each other at a corner. This particular combination helped him to create the optical illusion of dispersed structural weight.[54] Le Corbusier attached great importance to color, and on many occasions treated color in architecture as an end and not just simply a means. The symbolic meanings of color were of no less significance to him. The relationship between polychromatism and monochromatism are considered an important dialectical part of Le Corbusier's architecture.[55]

---

53. Scott, *Architecture of Humanism*, 229.
54. Rasmussen, *Experiencing Architecture*, 95–96.
55. Riley, *Color Codes*, 209.

SUMMING UP

Color in architecture is not an independent element. Its uses depend on architectural aesthetics as well as on concrete things: the functions of the building, its forms, the division of its interior spaces, its environment, and natural and artificial lighting. If one ignores these elements, it is impossible to create satisfying architecture that is appropriate from both the functional and aesthetic points of view. Any collection of laws, not only in architecture but also in other arts, is no guarantee of the final result, despite what artists at the end of the nineteenth century had expected when fueled by the promises of scientific and technological progress. According to the art historian Adrian Stokes, no single set of exhaustive rules explaining the principles of color harmony in art can determine the quality of the result attained by their application. Despite the fact that there were many theoretical concepts about the usage and combination of colors, practice often goes beyond them. Stokes ironically remarked that such torturing methods were practiced far less zealously but much more effectively by the old masters.[56] Moreover, it well known that the practice of craft is one of the many requirements in any field of art. However, an appropriate usage and integrity of color application is expressed quite well in the parallel between dwellings and clothing offered by Frank Lloyd Wright, who said that when we are well-dressed in public we forget about our clothes; when we live in a beautiful environment we do not restrict our behavior, and do not reproach ourselves because of a lack of self-esteem, since the environment represents us such as we would like to look like.[57] In addition, Frank Lloyd Wright claimed that color in architecture ought to be subordinated to forms that exist in nature. Accordingly, he advised architects to study the natural colors of fields and forests, and to use the soft, warm optimistic tones of earth and autumn leaves instead of the pessimistic colors blue, purple, cold green, and gray, since he thought warm colors suited good decoration better.[58]

While analyzing aspects of architecture's perception, an illusion suggesting that the colors of an interior or an exterior awaken our immediate reactions might take over. However, the experience of architec-

---

56. Stokes, *The Image in Form*, 53.
57. Wright, *Writings and Buildings*, 34.
58. Wright, *On Architecture*, 22.

ture is a far more complex and complicated phenomenon. Of course, natural color as well as natural light produce an effect on our senses, but in discussing architecture we should distinguish between ordinary and "imaginative" perception, as suggested by the philosopher Roger Scruton, who insists that the experience of architecture is of the imaginative type. In his view, this fact should determine our understanding of buildings as well as our reaction to them.[59] He concludes that we perceive architectural buildings with the help of reasoning, memory, knowledge, and imagination, and that all these faculties contribute to transform our visual impressions. Thus, color in architecture is related to other elements, and cannot be treated as simply an emotional stimulant; it gives an experience that is related to intellectual experiences and evaluations.

---

59. Scruton, *Aesthetics of Architecture*, 74.

3

Architecture and Sound

CAN WE HEAR ARCHITECTURE? —Steen Eiler Rasmussen asked in his book *Experiencing Architecture*, and continued his meditation on the subject by providing a contrary argument: when asked such a question, many people would most probably conclude that architecture does not produce sound, so accordingly, it cannot be heard.[1] However, Rasmussen brought forward another argument—architecture does not radiate light, but nevertheless it can be seen; human beings are capable of seeing the light reflected by the buildings, and they can get an impression of its form and materials; thus it would be fair to conclude that the human ear hears the sounds reflected by architecture. To illustrate his point, the architectural theorist drew his readers' attention to the scenes of the classic British feature film *The Third Man*, directed by Carol Reed, where a pursued criminal takes flight in the dark tunnels of Vienna's sewers: the sound of his feet splashing in the water and the echo of the voices of the men who are chasing the fugitive in the tunnel allow the spectator to have an almost visual impression of where the action is taking place, despite the fact that they can hardly be seen. Rasmussen's remark was extremely to the point. One can recall numerous scenes from a variety of movies where the experience of architectural surroundings is generated by sound. Whenever I reread Rasmussen's insightful observations, I immediately recall another movie, *The Stalker*—a film by the Russian filmmaker Andrei Tarkovsky—where a mysterious, almost metaphysical reality is created not only visually, but with the help of sounds as well. Characters in this film—a tiny group of individuals accompanied by a

---

1. Rasmussen, *Experiencing Architecture*, 224.

guide called the "stalker"—enter an area called the Zone, where all human desires are supposed to be fulfilled. Dripping and running water, splashing feet, whispering, and other acoustic effects help to create an almost metaphysical atmosphere, adding to the visuals; the sound also allows the onlooker to imagine the spacious deserted buildings in which the action of the film takes place. Though we seldom consciously rely on hearing while experiencing architecture, it does not mean that the acoustic features of buildings remain outside human experience. Alas, in the modern era modulations of sound are obviously becoming less and less relevant in the architectural experience. This undeniable fact can be explained by the paradox of progress: humans create their own environment, and the environment in turn shapes humans. No wonder that while human dwellings are becoming more and more convenient and technologically sophisticated than in any other historical period, the contemporary human being loses the unmatched sensitivity to the natural environment possessed in prehistoric times, when the instinct of survival urged the development of vision and hearing. The rapid development of technologies that provide so many contemporary conveniences, without which we can hardly imagine everyday life, transformed and muffled the ability of an individual to directly sense his or her natural environment. Contemporary planners and designers of urban dwellings are much less concerned with the acoustical qualities of their buildings than their predecessors were. The pragmatic desire to guarantee a maximum of comfortability often overshadows any attempts to create an environment that could boast of various, not to mention unique, acoustic qualities, capable of providing special psychological and aesthetic effects. Monotony of sound and acoustic uniformity have become a constant state of contemporary architecture, removing the possibility of experiencing and living the pleasure provided by variety. But in older times the situation was quite different: every architectural structure, because of its inside arrangements, materials, constitution of spaces, and of course because of the experience and knowledge of its designer and builder, had its own acoustic character. Anyone who has ever visited Romanesque basilicas or vaulted Gothic cathedrals will never forget or mistake their sound. Even whispering voices echo in interior spaces amidst light pouring down through the stained glass windows, and capture our senses. The divine sounds of Gregorian chants emerge as if from the depths of the church, and touch our souls, preparing us for meditative contemplation . . .

MUSIC AND ARCHITECTURE IN ANTIQUITY

What is the nature of sound? This question was widely discussed in ancient Greece. Some early Greek thinkers maintained that a cosmic sound, or drone, is generated by the seven planets revolving around the Earth; however, man is unable to hear it because of earthly imperfection, so they made attempts to formulate mathematical rules that would convey the supernatural drone. No wonder the sages of the period gave so much consideration to music and sound as unearthly phenomenon. Esoteric quasi-philosophic movements like Orphism and Pythagoreanism came into being; their members maintained that music is a key to understanding the mysteries of the world. Orphism attributed a special mystical meaning to Orpheus, who had revealed the secrets of the gods to people with the help of music, and even competed with them in power of prophetic insight. Besides, it was thought that he was the first to convey to people the meaning of the rituals of initiation.[2] As there is no precise evidence, it is speculated that Orpheus lived in Thrace during the post-Homeric period, and it is he who reformed the ecstatic cult of Dionysus, converting it to the more ascetic and speculative branch of this ancient religion, which sought the same goal using other means—more conscious and intellectual ones.[3] He disseminated his doctrine in the vicinity of Croton in the second half of the sixth century B.C. After his death, Orpheus became a symbol of Greek wisdom, and as the object of a religious cult he was worshipped as a mythological being. When Orpheus was placed on the same footing as his teaching, he was considered a son of Apollo—a divine and perfect truth and Calypso—muse of harmony and rhythm. According to Manley P. Hall, Orphism is a secret doctrine, or Apollo revealed through music or Calypso.[4] Though the Orphic movement remained on the margins of Greek culture because of its esoteric character, some of the views disseminated by its adherents entered other antique doctrines; they were echoed in the cosmology of Pythagoras, who considered Orpheus his own guardian, and eventually found expression in the worldview of the Neoplatonists.

In the philosophy and religion of the Pythagoreans, special attention was given to the notion of world harmony—called "the music of

---

2. Guthrie, *Orpheus and Greek Religion*, 17.
3. Godwin, *Mystery Religions*, 144.
4. Hall, *Enciklopediceskoje*, 88.

the spheres" in ancient Greece. For Pythagorus, cosmos meant less an orderly or proportionate system and more harmony. In his teaching, the universe was interpreted as a gigantic one-stringed musical instrument; the upper part of the string stretched to absolute spirit (sky), and the lower part rested on absolute matter (earth). It is supposed that this musical one-string instrument, known as the monochord, was invented by Pythagoras himself. As one can hardly imagine such an instrument for producing sound, it is more likely that it was constructed as a means of producing analogies between sound and mathematics. Architectural historian George L. Hersey suggests that one should consider the monochord a "philosophical instrument," used to demonstrate the relationship between the height of musical tones and the physical intervals of musical instruments.[5] Although the well-known story, which relates that the relationship between number and sound was discovered by Pythagorus when he was passing by a smithy and took notice of the different sounds produced by the hammer, is lately dismissed by scholars as a version of an old Asiatic legend, Pythagoras undoubtedly conducted experiments with the monochord.[6] According to the testimony of Iamblichus, his great contemporary gained his esoteric knowledge while roaming in foreign countries: he was supposed to have been introduced to all the mysteries of Phoenicians; he knew the sacred rituals practiced in Syria; and spent a long time—no less than twenty-two years—in Egyptian temples, where he studied astronomy and geometry, and it was there that the secrets of gods were revealed to him.[7] The universe, Pythagoras claimed, was made of distinct parts, or spheres. However, different authors relying on different sources disagree about their exact number—whether there were seven or twelve still remains uncertain—particularly since the Pythagoreans themselves provide contradicting data. What raises no doubt is that seven planets moving in a different speed were located between the highest and lowest parts of the universe. The movement of these planets produced sound of a tone dependent on the size of the planet and the speed of its movement. They reasoned that the lowest tone belongs to Saturn, the highest is produced by the Moon. Seen from the Earth, the planets were located in this order: first was the Moon (Selena);

5. Hersey, *Architecture and Geometry*, 53–54.
6. Fideler, *The Pythagorean Sourcebook*, 24.
7. Iamblichus, "Life of Pythagoras," 60–61.

further—Mercury (Hermes); Venus (Aphrodite); Sun (Apollo); Mars (Arias); Jupiter (Zeus); and Saturn (Cronos). The distances between the planets were likened to musical intervals. In the Pythagorean cosmology, bodies of the sky had their earthly equivalents; thus the sound diffused by the seven planets was related to the seven vowels articulated by human beings. When the teaching of the Pythagoreans became consolidated, attempts were made to prove rationally that nature, man, and music are governed by the same laws. Since the imperfect human senses are unable to perceive them, it was suggested that one should rely on mathematical laws discovered by reason: when a sequence of numbers was established, it was used to analyze the relationships between the universe, the human body, and music. The Pythagorean sequence of numbers made from even (female) and odd (male) numbers, was ruled by a primeval, non-divisible element of being—the "monad," superior to any number. Abstract numbers also represented a physical body: one meant a dot; two a line; three a triangle; four a pyramid. According to the Pythagoreans, the structure of the world matched the fifth and sixth intervals of the octave—consonances. The relation of their proportions was expressed mathematically as 2:1, 3:2, and 4:3. Pythagoreans claimed that that the sequence of numbers 1+2+3+4=10 corresponded to divine variety. This was the formula upon which the entire act of the creation of the universe was based. The followers of this doctrine were most probably the first in so-called Western civilization to prove that there is a relationship between musical intervals and simple proportions.[8] As the musical octave is made out of seven intervals, the analogy between the structure of the cosmos and music becomes even more evident. This fundamental discovery encouraged the thinkers of antique Greece to look for equivalents between music and architectural proportions. Manley P. Hall has observed that Greek mysteries were based on the accordance of music and form. Architectural elements were to conform to musical notes, or to have musical analogies of their own. When a building made of these elements was erected, it resembled a musical chord, and was considered perfect on condition it conformed completely to the requirements of harmonious musical intervals.[9] The real impact of Pythagoras on the theory of harmony is an open question, for he, like many other ancient sages, left no written documenta-

---

8. Haase, "Harmonics in Architecture," 93.
9. Hall, *Enciklopediceskoje*, 294.

tion of his thinking. But undoubtedly the Pythagorean tradition was closely related to the secret teaching of which, however, only fragments survived. Architectural historian Rudolf Haase claims that certain conditions in ancient times forced the Pythagoreans to keep their teaching secret. There were several mysterious cults that relied heavily on vows of secrecy. To disclose the secrets of their teaching meant death for the violator. Haase draws our attention to the fact that there was at least one recorded case of this punishment. It is generally believed that these strict vows prevented information about Pythagorean concepts from reaching a wider audience.[10] This line of thinking can be traced in the writings of the British historian of philosophy Bernard Bosanquet, who emphasized at the end of the nineteenth century that

> It is hard to elicit much of definite historical fact from the traditions that refer to early Pythagoreanism. It seems certain, however, on the authority of Aristotle, that Philosophers known as Pythagoreans had pursued mathematical investigations with success, but had interpreted some of their results after the manner of mysticism. It is also definitely asserted that numerical relations of the musical scale were discovered by them.[11]

Contemporary researchers into the philosophy of antiquity, although they do not question the Pythagorists' contribution to the study of harmony, have a much more skeptical attitude towards their achievements in mathematics, and refer to the critical remarks found in the writings of Aristotle regarding the concept of the "harmony of things" prophesied by the Pythagorean Philolaus.[12] Without getting further into discussions of specialists on this issue, I will go further to suggest that echos of Pythagorean teaching can be found in Plato's philosophy, especially in his last treatises, where he distances himself from the ideas expressed in his early writings. For example, in *Hippias Major* he still emphasized the sensual aspect of aesthetic experience, claiming that beauty is what is seen and heard, what provides pleasure to human senses and, accordingly is useful, i.e., serves goodness. In his last and most mysterious piece of writing—*Timaeus*, explaining the beauty of images and sounds—Plato says:

---

10. Haase, "Harmonics in Architecture," 94–95.
11. Bosanquet, *A History of Aesthetics*, 46.
12. Barnes, *The Presocratic Philosophers*, 392–95.

> God devised the gift of sight for us so that we might observe the movements which have been described by reason in the heavens, and apply them to the motions of our own mind, which are akin to them, so far as what is troubled can claim kinship with what is serene. For so we might learn a lesson, and by entering into the ideal nature of that design and imitating the perfect patterns set by God might adjust thereto our own random motions. And the same holds for good for voice and hearing; the gods bestowed them on us for the same end and purpose. . . . And so far the as vocal music goes, it is given to us to be heard for the sake of melody. And melody, since its movements are related to the changes of our own souls, is to be valued, if a man use his mind in art, not for irrational pleasure, as is the fashion now; rather it is given us to help us in ordering and assimilating to it the discordant motions of our souls.[13]

It can be rightly concluded that in this concept of sound and hearing, Plato turned back to the Pythagorean understanding of harmony, stressing that there is a correspondence between the structure of form and sound. Cosmos, according to this great mind, has two essential features: musicality and concord. Thus it is made as a musical instrument of extraterrestrial origin, and the golden section is the basis of its harmony. The measure called the golden section corresponds to a harmonious proportion, and besides this one there exists arithmetic and geometric proportion.

This tradition of thinking was further elaborated by later Greek philosophers of the Hellenistic period. Plotinus, who revived the school of Platonic thinking, took Pythagorean ideas seriously. Though he dismissed beauty's dependence on formal symmetry, claiming that beauty is made not only out of relations between parts—for example, he thought that color is beautiful as such, and its beauty has nothing to do with proportions between parts—he nevertheless agreed that the beauty of sound can be measured using mathematical numbers. According to Plotinus, those modes of sounds that do not reach the ear, by creating those modes that can be heard, urged the human soul to understand beauty in showing where the idea is hidden; thus sensual sounds should be measured with the help of numbers. But only a principle that enables the idea to come into being by overcoming the material is to be applied.[14] In other words, the theory of harmony formulated by Pythagoras and

---

13. Plato, *Timaeus*, 65.
14. Plotinus, *Enneads*, 303.

his followers, which managed to remain alive long after the Pythagorean school of thought had disintegrated, found expression in Neoplatonic doctrines of the Hellenistic epoch. Its echoes can be traced even in the writings of later British philosophers, who revived and sustained Neoplatonic thinking. This tradition is perhaps best represented by the writings of George Berkeley and his fellows at Cambridge University.

Plotinus meditated on the origin of sound, asking whether a sound could come into being if two bodies collide with each other without any intermediate through which it could reach human senses. According to Plotinus, air is essential, because without its vibration there would be no sound at all. But if air is the main condition, and if sound is created by air movement exclusively, how can one explain the differences in voices and other sounds? Noticing that bodies of different natures spread different sounds (for example, when a bronze body hits another bronze item we hear a different sound than the one when it hits an object of another material), Plotinus concluded that air is not essential for sound to come into being; sound is produced when hard bodies collide, and it is this collision that reaches our senses as sound. Macrobius, who lived in the fourth century A.D. and was especially esteemed during the Middle Ages, in summing up the cosmological doctrines of the Neoplatonists concluded that the Soul of the Universe, which brought the body of cosmos into movement, had to be related to those numbers that created musical harmony, in order to harmonize the sound affected by its accelerating impulse.[15] Relying for guidance on the "wise and truthful" statements of Cicero, Macrobius argued that while accelerating the movement of the spheres, the Soul of the Universe created tones separated by uneven but clearly settled intervals of proportions, corresponding to the primary material of creation. These strictly proportioned intervals appeared in the bodily cosmos out of the material of the Soul, and gave birth to harmony.[16] Vitruvius—one of the greatest authorities throughout the medieval period—became the most frequently cited pre-Christian author on principles of Pythagorean harmony, accommodating them to practical use in architecture. His architectural theory grew on the foundations of the doctrine of proportions: architectural structure was understood as a harmonious relationship between the parts and the whole, and as a well-composed interaction of elements based on the rules of mathemat-

15. Godwin, *The Harmony of the Spheres*, 65.
16. Ibid., 69.

ics and geometry. In his treatise *De Architectura Libri Decem*, following Aristoxenus, he gave a concise presentation of the essence of Pythagorean harmony and discussed how to guarantee proper proportions and the acoustical unity of architectural buildings. Vitruvius claimed that while building a theater, the architect must choose a place that is not "deaf," i.e., he should take into consideration the natural qualities of the site, choosing one that enables the voice to disperse in space freely, without any obstruction. Using the analogy of ripples in the water, Vitruvius explained it thusly:

> Voice is a flowing breath of air, perceptible to hearing by contact. It moves in an endless number of circular rounds like the innumerably increasing circular waves which appear when a stone is thrown into smooth water, and which keep on indefinitely from the centre unless interrupted by narrow limits, or by some obstruction which prevents such waves from reaching their end in due formation... In the same manner the voice executes its movements in concentric circles; but while in the case of water the circles move horizontally on a plane surface, the voice not only proceeds horizontally, but also ascends vertically by regular stages.[17]

He drew his readers' attention to the fact that ancient architects took a very serious attitude toward the laws of nature, and thus they perfected the arrangement of the audience's lines in the theater, studied the ascendance of voice according to the "canonical theory of the mathematicians and that of the musicians." These sources urged them to model the architectural space of a theater so that nothing would obstruct the flowing voice. Vitruvius advised that the curved cross-aisles be constructed in proportions relative, it is thought, to the height of the theatre, but not higher than the footway of the passage in broad. If they are loftier, they will throw back the voice and drive it away from the upper position, thus preventing the case-endings of words from reaching with distinct meaning the ears of those who are in the uppermost seats above the cross-aisles.[18]

He demanded that an architect take special measures in order to ensure that a voice ascending the upper parts of the theatre from the stage would sound clearly and would not disperse in the air, and that each and every person would hear it. To assure the quality of the sound, Vitruvius recommended using bronze vessels installed in specially des-

---

17. Vitruvius, *The Ten Books on Architecture*, 138–39.
18. Ibid., 138.

ignated places in niches. These vessels had to be placed bottoms up and an interval of two and a half feet had to be allowed between them and the nearest viewer; the number and location of the vessels had to be adjusted to the size of the theatre, and to correspond to the sequence of the height of note. "On this principle of arrangement, the voice, uttered from the stage as from a centre, and spreading and striking against the cavities of the different vessels, as it comes in contact with them, will be increased in clearness of sound, and will wake an harmonious note in unison with itself," Vitruvius claimed.[19] In those cases where a theatre is extremely large, he advised dividing its height into four parts; three horizontal rows of niches should be constructed, each devoted to produce "enharmonic," "chromatic," and "diatonic" sound.[20] The arrangement of the vessels had to correspond to the so-called Greek gradation of notes. These precise remarks show that the author of the renowned treatise was not only versed in musical theory, but also had sufficient practical knowledge of the mechanics of acoustics. This is witnessed by his further suggestion that in those cases where materials that have no qualities of reverberation are used for building theaters—for example, stone—the builder should take into consideration the principles of *echea* discovered by Greek mathematicians and musicians.

NUMBER, SOUND, AND ARCHITECTURE IN THE MIDDLE AGES

Medieval authors, appealing to Vitruvius' authority, based their aesthetic theories on the importance of proportions and numbers for the experience of beauty and things considered beautiful. In the early medieval period, this path was chosen by two important Christian thinkers of the fifth century—St. Aurelius Augustine and Boethius. Both influential philosophers, while developing further the ideas introduced in antiquity, strongly emphasized numbers and proportions. The German architectural historian Otto Georg von Simson pointed out that to Augustine, music and architecture were sisters, because both of them were considered daughters of the number, thus both of them are equally noble, as architecture reflects eternal harmony while music reveals it through

---

19. Ibid., 143.
20. Ibid., 144.

echo.[21] Boethius, however, ascribed music to the sciences, and was deeply convinced that sounds are subordinate to numbers; he claimed that the construction of nature, human beings, and the cosmos is based on the same principles of numbers and proportions. Explaining this dependency, he applied an analogy: a human being viewing a triangle or quadrangle recognizes these geometric figures with no difficulty, but in order to understand their nature he must turn to mathematics.[22] Supporting his thesis with Pythagorean cosmology, he argued that number and sound are closely interrelated; giant heavenly bodies that move around the earth produce a sound that does not reach human ears; thus it can only be understood by the human mind. According to Boethius, there are three kinds of music:

> The first kind, the cosmic, is discernible especially in those things which are observed in heaven itself, or in the combination of elements or the diversity of seasons. For how can it happen that so swift a heavenly machine moves on a mute and silent course? Although that sound does not penetrate our ears—which necessarily happens for many reasons—it is nevertheless impossible that such an extremely fast motion of such large bodies should produce absolutely no sound, especially since the course of the stars are joined by such harmonious union that nothing so perfectly united, nothing so perfectly fitted together, can be realized.[23]

He considered the humane *musica humana* and *musica instrumentalis* only a shadow of *musica mundana* (the music of cosmic spheres). And the latter is no more than an almost inaudible echo of nine choirs of angels. And although we human beings can not hear heavenly music because of our imperfection, we are by nature related to the cosmos, and experience contemplation of beauty by discovering mathematical relations and understanding the dependency of the world on them. This discovery, according to Boethius, awakens a real sense of beauty. Not all evaluations should be left to human senses, even if hearing gives rise to musical art. So he considered hearing a kind of primary impulse; but abilities such as perfection and recognition lie within the human mind. The mind, since it is governed by certain rules, is never wrong as far as

21. Simson, *The Gothic Cathedral*, 23.
22. Ovsianikov, *Istorija estetiki*, 249.
23. Boethius, *Fundamentals*, 9.

judgement is concerned. The Pythagoreans, he maintains, distrust the human ear and consequently take the "middle of the road." They decipher the sounds with the help of hearing, but study and calculate them with "rules and reason." His own belief is that the senses should be subjected to reason.[24] Rejecting sensual values as temporary and misleading, the thinker concluded that the musician is nothing more than a theorist who studies the mathematical laws of sound. Renowned Italian scholar Umberto Eco has justly remarked that to Boethius, the musician is the one who judges music using the mind, and one can understand why he hailed Pythagoras, who set out to study music rejecting the "estimations of ear"; thus his attitude toward musical experience is the attitude of the scientist, so typical in the early medieval phase.[25]

The identification of music with science was institutionalized: musical theory was taught in medieval university programs among the seven liberal arts (*septem artis liberalis*) as an essential discipline, equal to mathematics and astronomy. Boethius, in the same way as Aristotle before him, was convinced that music influences not just hearing, but also the human soul—certain rhythms and melodies help to reinforce the morality of a human being. He concluded that the state of the human body and soul is ruled by the same proportions that unite and attune "harmonious modulations." For both St. Augustine and Boethius—authors who created the outlines of the medieval concept of beauty—music's dependence on number was a foundation of a quantitative aesthetic doctrine. The issue of proportions and the symbolism of numbers was further developed by later medieval thinkers, including Vincent of Beauvois and Hugh of St. Victor. The latter, while enumerating the three kinds of music:—cosmic, human, and instrumental—was diligently following the dogmas established earlier by Boethius.[26] An anonymous contemporary of Hugh of St. Victor repeated the same division of music into these three kinds in his treatise, and claimed that the music of the universe is made by the four elements and units of time, as well as higher (supernatural) bodies. This was titled the golden series or the measure of threefold harmony, i.e., octave, quinta, and quarta. Human music is made from the harmony of humanity and the so-called union of four inclinations, as well as the body and soul. Instrumental

24. Ovsianikov, *Istorija estetiki*, 254.
25. Eco, *Art and Beauty in the Middle Ages*, 30.
26. Hugh of St. Victor, *The Didascalicon*, 69.

music is made of rhythms laid out in adequate proportions of sound and number.[27] Johannes Scotus Eriugena, who lived in 815–877, interpreted cosmic harmony in a rather original way. According to him, the Moon, Sun, Saturn, and the stars circle around the Earth, while Venus, Mars, and Jupiter circle around the Sun. This meant that there were fixed distances between the Earth, Sun, and the sphere of the stars, and the theory of planetary music had to take into account the possibility of shifting tone. It could be said that Eriugena was the first thinker who, contrary to his predecessor musical theorists, interpreted harmony not as fixed and static, but as a dynamic and shifting phenomenon.

The analogy between music and architecture in the Middle Ages was expressed in philosophical metaphors. When philosophers described God as an artistic architect (*elegans architectus*), who converted the whole universe into his palace and harmonized all of creation with the help of musical proportions, a specific architectural practice followed.[28] After the Gothic era dawned, numerous theoretical explanations covering the essence of proportions and offering laws for various branches of art were applied to architecture as well. The research conducted by Rudolf Haase, mentioned earlier in this chapter, as well as the studies of other authors, allow us to conclude that Gothic architecture was clearly designed according to the laws of musical proportions. While the Gothic cathedral is divided into squares according the laws of proportions known to the old masters, the square lying on the bottom was divided into squares that grew proportionately smaller, and each of these, when turned 45 degrees, can be placed into one another. This was the Gothic canon, and it was widely applied in the structure of cathedrals. Each part of the building was measured by applying this system of squares. It was also widely used to draw the proportions of towers. The relation of all architectural segments in this system of squares was 1:2—precisely what makes a series of octaves. Thus it is possible to say that the structure of architecture during the period was based on musical analogy.[29]

---

27. The Anonymous of St. Emmeram, *De Musica Mensurates*, 67.
28. Kostof, "The Architect in the Middle Ages," 79.
29. Haase, "Harmonics in Architecture," 105.

MUSICAL HARMONY IN RENAISSANCE ARCHITECTURE

There were numerous conceptual attempts to develop a system of architectural proportions based on the principles of musical harmony. Reconsideration of classical culture urged interest not only in the forms and shapes of antique architecture, but also in treatises where its structural principles were provided. Pythagorean cosmological theory and the search for harmonious proportions in architecture became an object of intellectual discussion. Philosophers and humanists as well as musical theorists reconsidered a notion of harmony as passionately as these issues were treated in antique Greece. In his treatise "On the Dignity of Man," philosopher Pico de Mirandola discussed the bonds uniting Orphic and Pythagorean thinkers. Basing his outlook on the testimony of Iamblichus, he demonstrated that Pythagoras used Orphic theology as a model when creating his philosophical system. According to Pico, Pythagoras's maxims were treated as sacred because they were based on the principles of Orpheus. He also stated that everything that was monumental or divine in Greek philosophy sprang from this "primary source."[30] Pico argued that both the Pythagoreans, and earlier Orpheus, kept the secrets of their dogmas by enveloping them in poetic form. Florence's humanist Marsilio Ficino, who translated the most important sources of Platonism and Neoplatonism, discussed the relations between music and soul. Both a song and soul are able to cross the borders between the material and non-material worlds; thus, invisible images influence the ethos and can be comprehended. Harmony, concentrated in a human being, envelopes all of the cosmos, that is to say, the microcosmos reflects the macrocosmos. Ficino claimed that in this common order all things, despite their variety, once again become unified according to a single harmony and a rational plan.[31] The musical theorist Zarlino, in his treatise "Institutioni harmoniche," agreed, asking that if the world were created by God in such a harmonious way, why should one not think that this also applies to a human being. Moreover, contemplated Zarlino, if the soul of the world is harmony, how can it be that our soul should not be the cause of all this harmony of ours, and why should it not be joined to our body. He considered this reasoning sound because the Almighty created man

---

30. Pico de Mirandola, "On the Dignity of Man," 253.
31. Ficino, *Renaissance Philosophy*, 195.

according to a larger plan called Cosmos.[32] Another musician of this period, Franchino Gafurio, stressed the influence of Pythagoras on the relationship between mathematics, music, and geometry, and saw the sound that is produced by cosmic bodies as a result of motion:

> Indeed, these celestial bodies and the corresponding elements, mixed together simultaneously by a certain combination of consonance, completed this whole universe. This universe is called 'mundus' by philosophers, because it is always in motion. They do not believe that he—the highest and best creator and builder of all things—perfected such a great and so very significant machine to be motionless in useless and inapt taciturnity, that anything was missing to complete this most ornate of all works, so that the work would resound harmoniously and bring forth many agreements of sounds.[33]

To Gafurio it was simply unbelievable that such a vast heavenly mechanism could move quietly and silently. Thus he claimed that the soul of the universe joins its cosmic body in certain harmonious proportions. This theory echos the thoughts of Boethius. The Pythagorean system was also passionately defended by the musical theorist Vincenzo Galilei, father of the great dissenting scholar whose findings made a revolutionary breakthrough in astronomy. The treatise of Vitruvius, which is considered the most authoritative and detailed theoretical account of the Roman art of building, became a primary source from which the architects of Renaissance paid tribute to classical architectural principles, used for drawing ideas and inspirations as well as for approval of architectural practice. The architecture treatise of Leon Battista Alberti reflects a Vitruvian influence in the very title of his book—*De re aedificatoria libri decem;* this did not, however, restrain his dispute with his great predecessor. Alberti was a practicing architect as well as a theorist, and he produced architectural plans according to his own principles of harmony and proportion. The Church of St. Francis in Rimini is a surviving structure reflecting his theoretical doctrine. Another great Renaissance builder, Andrea Palladio, was well acquainted with the treatises of these theorists, but also delved into the musical principles of ancient Greek architecture. There is evidence that a French architectural theorist, Phillibert Delorme, in his treatise *Premier tome de'l architecture,* tried to prove that

---

32. Tomlinson, *Metaphysical Song*, 12.
33. Gafurio, *The Theory of Music*, 30.

the French needed to have their own national architectural order, as the Corinthians once did, and he was planing to write a volume with the goal of tuning classical theory and Christian number symbology. He was, however, unable to complete this endeavor for unknown reasons.[34] Renaissance painters were also deeply interested in the principles of classical musical harmony. Erwin Panofsky has noted that the art of Venice is based not only on color and peculiarities of brush-work, but on musical harmony as well. He drew attention to a curious and interesting detail: the representatives of Venice school—Bembo and Betussin—created an ear, but not an eye, as an engine of spiritual beauty and love; even this kind of thinking contradicted the orthodoxies of the period.[35]

Rudolf Wittkower, who has provided a thorough and detailed account of the architectural principles of Renaissance period, emphasized the importance of harmony in architectural practice. The architects of the period, who relied heavily on the authority of Vitruvius, believed that the external and internal structure of a building must be measured according to mathematical relations, and also reflect the proportions of a human body. One of these authors reasoned that since man is an image of God, and since the proportions of his body were settled by divine will, architectural proportion should represent this cosmic order.[36] Architectural theorists searching for principles of the harmony of proportions turned to ancient Greek, and especially Pythagorean, thinkers. Wittkower provided evidence that in the fifteenth century, an interest in Pythagorean and Platonic doctrines of harmony was maturing in Europe; Italy in particular, but not exclusively. One of the examples provided by Wittkower is the Franciscan monk Francesco Giorgio, who published a treatise on the harmony of the universe in 1525, and a decade later, in 1534, was hired to draft a memorandum about the church of St. Francis in Venice, designed by Jacopo Sansovino. The monk claimed that the interior spaces of the edifice should be based on divine number three; the width of the nave should consist of nine lengths, its length of 27 lengths, because, as he suggested, neither Plato nor Aristotle mentioned a larger number when discussing the structure of the world. However, significance was attached not to numbers as such, but to their proportions, as theorists reasoned that the microcosmos is based on cosmic

---

34. Kostof, *The Architect in the Middle Ages*, 152.
35. Panofsky, *Studies in Iconology*, 148.
36. Wittkower, *Architectural Principles*, 101.

relations.[37] Research into the subject done by Wittkower proved the connection between this thinking and Pythagoras's discovery that tones can be measured in space, because musical consonances are conditioned by small even numbers. Giorgio also argued that the mathematical proportions of an interior space should be reflected in the central part of the façade. Wittkower concludes that Andrea Palladio, who belonged to later generation of Renaissance masters, was well aware of Giorgio's memorandum, and this was his source for the mysterious number 27, which he used for the proportions of the façade.[38] Of special interest is the curious fact that the memorandum written by a Franciscan monk was given for further evaluation to the painter Titian, the architect Serlio, and to the famous but later almost forgotten humanist Fortunio Spira. And all three experts in their own fields found this memorandum equally acceptable. Wittkower notes that the issue of proportions in architecture was not reserved for architects only: the unity between art and science of the day made every educated person an expert.[39] Andrea Palladio, in a treatise on architecture, provided rules for a system of orders; however, he made little mention of principles of harmony, obviously because he was treating them as common knowledge. In discussing the sizes of interior spaces, he stated that when the width and length of a room is six and twelve feet, its height should be nine feet; if the room is four and nine feet, its height should be six; in the case where the width and length is six and twelve, then the height should be eight feet. Wittkower concludes:

> In his exposition Palladio sticks to the practical side of the *metier* without mentioning what these proportions really signify. In actual fact, in these three examples the height of the room represent the arithmetic, geometric and 'harmonic' means between each of the two extremes. These three types of proportion are traditionally attributed to Pythagoras and without them no rational theory of proportion can be imagined.[40]

Though Palladio did not discuss principles of mathematical harmony, his treatise contains hints that practicing architects should follow them. In the first chapter of his first book, Palladio agreed with Vitruvius's statement that an edifice should meet three requirements: first it should be

37. Ibid., 103.
38. Ibid., 106.
39. Ibid.
40. Ibid., 109.

useful; secondly, be of long duration; and thirdly, it should be beautiful, because if these three are violated a building cannot be called acceptable. He explained that beauty consists of a beautiful form and concord between the whole and its parts, because a building should look like each separate part is needed for the sake of the whole.[41] Palladio enumerates and describes the seven most beautiful and most proportionate types of rooms: their form should be round or square, in which case the length should be equal to the diagonal of a square, and width to the edge of the square; or the room should be a square plus one-third of its size, square plus half of its size, or square plus two-thirds of its size; or it could make two squares.[42] Among the examples of edifices included in Palladio's treatise are those that contain not only numbers of the musical scale of ancient Greece, but also those of the Renaissance. Overviewing Palladian proportions, Wittkower draws our attention to another theorist of the period, Daniele Barbaro, who insisted that the rules of arithmetic unite music and astrology, because all material things have common and universal proportions. Palladio also argued that the proportions of sound and space are closely related, thus he had to believe in the universal value of a harmonious system.[43] Leon Battista Alberti formulated principles of proportions with even greater clarity. He indicated his indebtedness to musicians in describing the rules of harmonious relationships, which he called *finitio*. He noticed that musicians know them well, since nature reveals itself through harmony in the most perfect and complete way.[44] Alberti enumerated the numbers that condition harmonious relations: nature is based upon the principle of the triad; the number five governs many things; the divine number seven indicates the seven planets, the glory of creation, development, and maturity; among the uneven numbers, nine is also important because it reflects the heavenly spheres. Even numbers bear their own importance. As Alberti puts it:

> some philosophers maintain that the fourfould is consecrated to divinity, and that the most solemn oaths should be based on it. The sixfold is one of the very few which is called "perfect," because it is the sum of all its integral divisors. It is clear that the eightfold exerts a great influence on Nature. Those born in the

41. Palladio, *Cetyre knigi ob architekture v dvux tomach*, 1:1.
42. Ibid., 1:21.
43. Wittkower, *Architectural Principles*, 132.
44. Ibid., 110.

eight month will not survive, we have observed, except in Egypt. Among even numbers ten is the most important, since Aristotle called it "most perfect number of all."[45]

Alberti had no intention of giving a philosophical explanation of numbers, modestly stating that he only writes about matters important to an architect; however, he noticed that harmony is a mode of several sounds that are pleasant to the hearing: some tones are deep, others lasting, and the relationship between the two produces all manner of harmony.[46]

The concept of the musical structure of the world is reflected in the illustrations used in treatises that appeared during The Renaissance. Principles of cosmic harmony were based on allusions to the muses, who were considered the guardians of the planets. A treatise by Gafurio, *Practica musicale*, published in Milan in 1496, was illustrated with engravings where the cosmological theory of musical tones (and in fact the world's musicality) was told through visual images. In one of these engravings, Apollo is depicted on the edge of heaven, and a snake with three heads under his feet curls downwards toward the earth, which is surrounded by fire, air, and water. The names of musical tones are placed on the snake's body as if they were strings of a lyre, while muses and their corresponding planets are placed at the ends of the strings. In the illustrations of Tarot cards of the period, Apollo is usually given a double role as guardian of the muses and ruler of the planet. This interpretation of the structure of the cosmos is believed to go back to pre-Christian times.[47] Images like these were widespread at the time, and they bear witness to how thoroughly Renaissance minds were captured by the cosmology of antiquity. This Renaissance fascination continued, as later mythological reference books dedicated a lot of pages to mythical beings associated with the concept of the harmony of the universe. In a reference book by Natale Conti entitled *Ten books on Mythology or the Explanations of Fables*, published in 1551, or another by Vincento Cartari—*Images of Gods of the Ancient People*, published in 1556—the engravings convey cosmological conventions of the Greeks, putting a special emphasis on Apollo, the god of the sun, whose cult gained special importance during the discussed period. Publications of this kind were not just illustrations of the truths of antiquity, but also reflections on the moral beliefs of the

45. Alberti, *On the Art of Building*, 304.
46. Ibid., 305.
47. Seznec, *The Survival of Pagan Gods*, 140–41.

period.⁴⁸ Apollo was also very often personified in operas. In the opera *Orpheus*, composed by Claudio Monteverdi (1607), Apollo, as if *deux ex machina*, suddenly comes down to the earth in the last act, bringing harmony to the earth and the human soul.⁴⁹ Even these few random examples testify to the very close relations between music, mythology, and cosmology in nurturing ideas of universal harmony.

ANALOGIES BETWEEN ARCHITECTURE AND MUSIC IN THE POST-RENAISSANCE PERIOD

The idea of the correspondence between sound and cosmos was further developed in the Baroque epoch. The English alchemist and member of the Order of Rosicrucians Robert Fludd, in his treatise *Utriusque Cosmi*, explained the musical arrangement of the cosmos. According to Fludd, a monochord (a philosophical instrument devised by Pythagoras) is an internal principle, which, being in the center of the universe, harmonizes the entire life of the cosmos. He treats his heavenly instrument as made of upper (ideal and active) and lower (material and passive) octaves, which in turn are divided into fourths and fifths. The principle of light comes down to dark material in these intervals, and in the spot where they encounter each other, the sun acquires the power of change. His contemporary Jesuit and mystic Athanasius Kircher reasoned in a similar way: he notes that consonance and dissonance condition the harmony and order of the cosmos. He imagined God as the creator and player of an organ. Those six days during which, according to the Bible, the world was created were compared to the six registers of the cosmic organs. According to Kircher, both earthly and heavenly spheres can be divided into octaves.⁵⁰ Having accepted and revised several ideas of Robert Fludd and Johannes Kepler, he explained the harmony of the planets by using images of a "choir" and "symphony" designating the place taken by each heavenly body. Kircher further notes that Saturn, Jupiter, and Mars sing in the highest voice, and Jupiter (the consonance) always restrains and weakens Mars and Saturn (the dissonances). The Sun continues the middle part in perfect consonance, and she is always an octave away from the Earth, which is the bass; Venus, Mercury, and

---

48. Tomlinson, *Metaphysical Song*, 29–30.
49. Ibid., 3.
50. Roob, *Alchemy and Mysticism*, 274.

the Moon sing a hypatodon, while Venus and the Moon take hold of Mercury's intermediate dissonance and mollify him, converting into a consonance. Earth, the lowest of all, gets consonances and dissonances mixed together, and in this way a "perfect planetary music" is formed.[51] Kircher notes that planets revolve around their centers in an eccentric way, approaching and withdrawing, changing their positions toward the Zodiac, and together creating new variants of harmony, all of which occurs according to the laws of nature.

When the Renaissance infatuation with the legacy of Antique ideas, exotic ancient solar cults, and mystery started to crumble with the advent of the Baroque, and eventually gave way to purely rationalistic reasoning, metaphysical cosmological concepts gave way to reasoning based on a scientific knowledge of nature. Accordingly, interest in Pythagorean musical harmony and the principles of architectural proportions embedded in this kind of thinking slowly but resolutely faded. However, Johannes Kepler (1571–1630), the renowned German mathematician and astronomer, made an attempt to revive the Pythagorean tradition and to test its truthfulness by making it a life project (it is interesting to note that his astronomical discoveries were a side-effect of this more grand endeavor). He mentioned the idea of the Pythagorean harmony of the spheres in his letters of 1559, most probably inspired by Plato's *Republic*.[52] Kepler firmly believed that the mysteries of the universe can be discovered by understanding how musical tones related to planets. The speed of the planet correlated to the height of tone: the faster planets revolve, the higher the note reached; and those planets that revolve at a slower speed correspond to the basic register in a chorus. The scholar maintained the opinion that the speed of Saturn's revolution is equal to three, Jupiter's—four, Mars's—five, Earth's—ten, Venus's—twelve, and Mercury's—sixteen. The revolutions of Jupiter and Mars make an octave, while those of Saturn and Earth a major sixth and an octave put together. Together, the revolution of the planets sounds like a heavenly symphony created by God. Kepler claimed that

> Therefore there can be different sounds, but unless there is a definite order among them, which is defined by definite proportions, as a matter of mathematics, there will be no harmony among the parts. On the other hand, if the sound is taken away, what har-

51. Godwin, *The Harmony of the Spheres*, 274.
52. Kepler, *The Harmony of the World*, 19.

mony between the configurations could be derived. Furthermore, as musical harmony is not a sound, but order among several sounds, it follows from that it is in the category of relations. For the order of which we are speaking here is in relation, and the things which are ordered are related to each other.[53]

However, when the rational scientific attitude began to dominate, concepts of universal harmony lost their previous topicality, and finally fell into oblivion for several centuries. Only in the nineteenth century was this almost forgotten theme revived by the eccentric German scholar, a connoisseur of old Greek, Hebrew, Chinese and hieroglyphics, Albert von Thimmus, who published his findings in a book called *Harmonic Symbolism of Classical Antiquity*. However, because of his specific, difficult language and impenetrable discourse, as well as numerous references to sources in "exotic" languages, his research remained unknown to a wider scholarly audience. But the history of ideas is full of paradoxes and contradictions: outdated, dead doctrines sentenced to remain archival material for the rest of time sometimes recover their former value if some curious mind sets out on a path that seems totally forgotten and neglected. Due to the efforts of the Austrian scholar Hans Kayser, a group of dedicated researchers once again revived interest in the theories of the Pythagoreans, Johannes Kepler, and Albert von Thimmus.[54] Kayser and his colleagues at the Vienna Academy of Music revived the study of the Pythagoreans and their followers, and established a center for research into musical harmony. He discovered traces of buildings whose structures were built according to the laws of musical harmony in southern Italy, where thousands years ago a school of Pythagoreans was active. After studying the ruins of three edifices in Peastum, he proved that these buildings were erected according to the principles of Pythagorean musical harmony. Bonds between modern science and forgotten theories of antiquity continue to be found. Renowned Russian chemist Dmitri Mendeleev asserted that the weight of atoms is ruled by principles of a musical character. Martin Kemp provides material about Mendeleev's findings in this field: the latter gave a lecture in 1869 London in honor of Faraday, during which he stressed that the experimental method of studying nature utilized old Pythagorean ideas.[55]

53. Ibid., 290.
54. Haase, "Harmonics in Architecture," 89.
55. Kemp, "In Praise of Model Making," 17.

It may seem that the period when architects applied the principles of musical harmony is long gone. However, the Pythagorean understanding of the musical composition of architectural structures periodically resurfaces from the depths of human history. It is well known that the Swiss-French architect Le Corbusier, who is credited both as a gifted visionary of architectural modernism and as the author of megalomaniac utopian urban plans, was almost obsessed with a search for *le modulor*, a tool that could guarantee perfect architecture, and was especially interested in the mysterious Pythagorean science. Attempts have been made to design modern buildings to satisfy the universal laws of nature and musical harmony—yet another Swiss architect of the last century, Andre Studer, undertook this quest with all seriousness.[56] Attempts of this kind remind one that there is a layer in the legacy of the past that still appeals to the artistic imagination and scholarly reasoning, and this layer is capable of giving a powerful impetus to architectural thinking by invoking the parallels between music and architecture. Few these days would call architecture "frozen music," as a German philosopher did a few centuries ago. Architect Eliel Saarinen has justly remarked that architecture is not music, neither "frozen" nor of any other kind. He stressed that architecture simply bases itself on fundamental laws of organic order, and consequently is based on the same principles as music or any other organically healthy phenomenon.[57] And this is why the parallels between both arts are still relevant. How could one forget Frank Lloyd Wright's pronouncement, in which he used a pleasing metaphor to describe this brotherhood: music is architect's dear friend, whose advice should be taken without hesitation.[58]

These remarks bring us back to the question of proportionality and balance, since both architecture and music are related to it. Attempts to solve the mystery of the universe are often related to the teaching of Pythagoreans, but as Anthony Aveni has remarked, all cultures of the world share the same quality—they attempt to seek balance and harmony no matter how geographically remote they are. In a penetrating essay, Aveni discusses the numerology of the Mayan civilization, and reveals that the Mayan people reasoned in the same way as the ancient Greeks, believing that the basic instruments of the universe's sounds are the Sun

---

56. Haase, "Harmonics in Architecture," 111.
57. Saarinen, *The City*, 68.
58. Wright, *On Architecture*, 41.

and the Moon. The third cosmic body—Venus, the best heard and the brightest of all—was especially significant, because they calculated that its cycle of 584 days resonates with the cycle of the seasons of the year (365 days), making up a perfect relation of two numbers—eight and five. Mayans also discovered that the cycle of Venus, which takes eight years, corresponds to the number of lunar months. As it is for all societies that base their time count on the repetition of natural phenomenon, euphonic concurrence with cyclical periods of nature was extremely important.[59]

A NOTE ON ARCHITECTURAL ACOUSTICS

In this essay I have attempted to provide an overview of the application of universal music structures to architecture, as well as this idea's historical roots. However, there is one more important aspect of relations between sound and architecture, namely acoustics. This is a far larger theme than a few paragraphs of this chapter can do justice to, but a passing glimpse into it should be provided.

It is well known that religious music during the medieval period was strongly related to architecture: its style and quality largely depended on a specially arranged architectural setting. The interior spaces of Christian churches were designed to perfect the sound and use it to its full potential. Relying on English architectural acoustics research, Danish architectural theorist Steeen Eiler Rasmussen discussed the old pre-Renaissance basilica of St. Peter in Rome—an edifice containing five naves with colonnades between them, whose acoustics were such that a priest could not speak to congregates in his usual voice without the sound dispersing before reaching the audience. After experimenting, a rhythmic recital or intonation was introduced. A priest would raise his voice and then lower it, raise and lower it again, so that the main vowels became audible in full clarity and eventually drowned, while others followed them as modulations. In this way, the clarity was assured. Rasmussen notes that in this way a text became a chant, and the huge edifice itself shaped a special musical experience. Gregorian chants were specially created to be performed in Rome's St. Peter's basilica.[60] Almost the same conclusion was reached by another esteemed specialist of acoustics, Leo L. Beranek, who was one of the first to systematically study the acoustics of the best musi-

---

59. Aveni, "Is Harmony at the Heart of Things?" 64–65.
60. Rasmussen, *Experiencing Architecture*, 230.

cal halls. He claims that it is no accident that Gregorian chants sound best when performed in halls whose acoustics are similar to those of medieval cathedrals: that is, where the duration of reverberation is from five to ten seconds. In the seventeenth century, Giovanni Gabrieli wrote slow tempo antiphonal music for a choir, adjusted to the acoustics of St. Mark's Basilica. Beranek's conclusion is that in the period between 1600 and 1900, i.e., during the Renaissance, Baroque, Classic and Romantic eras, there was a close link between the acoustics of the building and the music performed in it.[61] During the Baroque, orchestral music was usually performed in the halls that were not too large, and the walls were covered with cloth to absorb the sound. As a rule, small chamber orchestras played in this acoustic milieu, and it naturally strengthened the intimacy of the music. The duration of reverberation in these spaces was much smaller—up to 1.5 seconds. Religious music was not so closely associated with architectural setting in this period, as it was more often performed in the halls of palaces rather than in churches.[62]

There has been sufficient research carried out to allow us to conclude that the volumetric size of the building, as well as the qualities of the interior surface that reflect sound, has a significant and direct impact on the experience of sound. Rasmussen discusses an interesting example of to what degree changes in acoustic qualities of the same building influence its audibility and aesthetic character. The church of St. Thomas in Leipzig, where Johann Sebastian Bach worked as an organist, was originally constructed as a Gothic cathedral; however, after the Reformation, when it became a Lutheran church, a number of changes were implemented in its interior structure: the stone walls were covered with wooden plates and this implementation significantly shortened the duration of sound's reverberation. In addition, balconies were installed on the side walls for the families of the city council to use. Later wooden chairs were installed in the congregation hall as well. Because of the abundance of wood, the space acquired specific acoustic qualities which were especially favorable for performing the more complex sound of Baroque music. It has been stated that the duration of reverberation, originally six to eight seconds, was shortened to 2.5 seconds.[63] Although these changes (the wooden balconies, plates, and upholstery)

---

61. Beranek, *Music, Acoustics, and Architecture*, 44.
62. Ibid., 45–46.
63. Rasmussen, *Experiencing Architecture*, 231.

weren't planned in advance and came into being accidentally, a close relationship between the interior space and the music was formed. Even these few examples, selected to illustrate another kind of relationship between music and architecture than those previously discussed, allows a vision of the profound possibilities contained in this "union of the muses," as well as a knowledge of the wisdom of the past. Hope Bagenal once suggested that for the best acoustic effect when constructing or adapting religious buildings, it is wise to choose a clever example, and to know that some types of churches provide better acoustics than others. He urged choosing smaller basilicas or early Christian churches as models, as well as Dominican or medieval churches of the later period with completely covered wooden ceilings without transepts; he also suggested taking a close look at the smaller version of a church with a flat roof designed by Wren.[64] It is surprising to find to what a limited degree these reasonable and expert recommendations are applied these days in Europe and elsewhere, despite the fact that a number of new churches are still being erected in areas inhabited by Christian populations. The modern epoch, despite its dominating technological impulse, seems to have largely neglected and ignored the scale of emotional and aesthetic experiences that have the power to translate architecture and sound into a durable unique pleasure.

SUMMING UP

The bonds between architecture and sound have been established and have continued developing since the rise of the classical civilization of ancient Greece. Whatever we might think of the Pythagorean cosmology or the tradition of secret esoteric knowledge, the search for rhythm, proportionality, and harmony has, in various ways, affected architecture throughout the centuries. The fact that architecture can sound in either a metaphorical or a direct sense was known to the "Elders," and to some of their heirs in modern times. However, a suspicious attitude toward traditional wisdom and neglect for anything that is termed "unscientific" has largely impoverished our minds and experiences. Ignoring the acoustic qualities of edifices has deprived contemporary culture, and given rise to the deaf architectural structures mushrooming in East and West, North and South. During the past century there were few con-

---

64. Bagenal, *Practical Acoustics*, 135–36.

scious attempts to enrich human dwellings with acoustic variety or to sense the individual sound qualities of buildings and materials. It is a paradox, but the technological advancements in the sphere of sound have hardly affected the interiors of the houses in which we dwell, work, pray, or even experience the pleasures of music. Ancient architectural buildings, be they the ruins of antique theaters in the open air, Christian basilicas, Gothic cathedrals, or Classical halls, are much better adjusted to various musical performances and the experience of sound than most modern buildings—sadly, in many cases, even halls designed for musical performances. However, there may still be some room for hope that individuals and communities who feel the weight of deaf architecture will occasionally turn back for inspiration to the rich sources of the past when creating architecture with the capacity to produce sound to be heard.

4

Architecture and Water

LIFE WITHOUT WATER IS impossible on Earth. Although a human can endure a long period of starvation or cold, without access to a source of water he is condemned to perish. Perhaps it is because of this knowledge, provided by human experience, that water was always considered one of the most essential conditions for survival, and while reasoning about the structure of the world ancient thinkers treated water as the most important and primary element. Water is especially valued and saved in those areas where, because of climatic conditions, this resource remains scarce. The names given to particular water sources in ancient civilizations indicate its paramountcy. One of the largest rivers in present-day Iran or Persia was called Zayandeh—"the life giving"—in olden times. This river provided a plentitude of water, supplying many of the oases of the region. The ancient Egyptians who worshipped Osiris believed that their God not only taught them how to situate pieces of arable land, measure their limits, and collect the harvest, but also how to irrigate the fields with the help of water canals.[1] The people of ancient Egypt believed that the Earth floats on gigantic underground waters that give birth to all life in the world. They believed the sun arose from the waters, and even the gods were given birth by these waters. It is therefore not surprising that water was related to birth, purification, and rebirth in Egyptian culture. The importance attached to water is reflected by ancient sources of symbology. The symbol of water in ancient Egypt was a wavy line; the composition of three such lines designated the primary ocean and the primary material out of which

1. Krupp, *Echoes of the Ancient Skies*, 6.

the world originated. In ancient China, people believed that all life was produced by one and the same source—that is, water. The Chinese based earthly order on the number five, which was made from the four main directions and a center; in addition, they recognized five principles of movement, action, and change. This is partly reminiscent of the primary elements of the ancient Greeks, which included water, fire, metal, wood, and earth, but is more complex and dynamic.[2] References to the primacy of water are also found in Indian Vedic sources: this element is described as the most motherly substance, as at the beginning everything was like a sea in darkness. Water is considered a life sustaining source in India; it exists everywhere in nature, but it takes various forms and shapes. Since water has neither beginning nor end, it is eternal; thus it is the beginning and the end of all things on earth. Traditional cosmology claims that water, as the primary substance, provided forms and volumes to all liquid bodies. Researchers into symbology note that quicksilver and the liquid substance of the human body were called water by alchemists; however, modern psychology, influenced by Sigmund Freud and Carl Gustav Jung, saw a liquid body as a symbol of the subconscious. On the other hand, water was associated with wisdom as well—in Mesopotamian cosmology, the depths of water were compared to unlimited and objective wisdom.[3] In Iranian myths about the end of the world, water and fire were interpreted as powerful destructive and purifying elements. There is one more notion of water found in ancient cultures—it is an image of water running from an enormous opening that was called the vagina of the Earth.[4] In most ancient mythologies, water was considered as the opposite of order and civilized life: people tried to distance themselves from it, to overcome it and tame it, or to triumph over the giant bodies that inhabit water. Similar interpretations are found in pagan Nordic mythology. Icelandic writer Snorri Sturluson, who lived in the Christian era, referring to numerous pre-Christian sources in his own epic poems, explained the creation of the world as the pagan Vikings imagined it. He wrote that the heaven of the gods, Valhalla, is separated from the earth by a huge bridge—a trembling rainbow—and the disk of the earth is enveloped by a gigantic ocean, which is the dwelling place of Midgard

2. Ibid., 262.
3. Cirlot, *Dictionary of Symbols*, 364–65.
4. Dillistone, *Christianity and Symbolism*, 185.

Serpent.⁵ Sturluson's account of the end of the world contains this description: when the "time of the wolf" will approach, giant beasts will rebel against the gods and the final battle will take place: the Sun will become dark and the stars will disappear from the sky. However, finally the Earth will surface once again from the depths of the ocean, and the newly lit world will see the sunlight.⁶ This was how the ancient people imagined the eternal power of water.

NOTIONS AND TECHNOLOGIES OF WATER IN ANCIENT CIVILIZATIONS

From the evidence provided by some later thinkers of ancient Greece, we know that water was treated as the fundamental element in the theory of world's origin constructed by the Orphist Damascius, who lived about 480 A. D. Following earlier commentators, he claimed that according to Orphic doctrine, there initially existed only water and mud, and when these two elements were mixed together Earth came into being. Thus originally there were only two elements: water and earth. Many thinkers of ancient Greece maintained that water is one of four primary and essential elements. Thinking of this kind goes back to the teaching of Empedocles, who preached that there are four "roots" of all things. From later testimonies, we learn that the founders of the Milesian school, Thales and Hipo, maintained that water is the origin of things. Aristotle pointed out that Simplicius had already come to the same conclusion. They came to this conclusion by analyzing phenomenon with the help of the senses. They knew that heat is possible because of humidity, and that those forms of life that get dry die. Furthermore, they claimed that all seeds are humid, and the same can be said of food. Thus it is understandable why Thales insisted that water is the origin of everything on this earth.⁷ According to Thales, things make up unity, as all things came out of one and the same source. Aristotle argued that:

> Some think that those ancients who, long before the present generation, were the first to theologize, had a similar idea of nature; because they presented Ocean and Tethys as the parents of becoming, and water as that by which the gods swore, which

---

5. Bronsted, *Vikings*, 271.
6. Ibid., 273.
7. Aristotle, *Works*, 23, 21.

these people styled the "Styx." For what is oldest and most honorable, and what anyone swears by is most honorable. Although it may not be clear whether this opinion about nature is primitive and ancient, Thales at any rate is said thus to have explained the principles and origins of things.[8]

The origin of things was an important object of reflection among many Greek philosophers of the ancient period. Anaximenes had a different opinion: according to him nature was a product of air; when air became rarefied, fire came into being; when it grew thicker, wind, clouds and water appeared, and later earth, stones and hard bodies started to exist. Earlier than Aristotle, Plato described the origin of things as being based on four essential elements: earth, water, air, and fire. He explained the interaction of elements as follows:

> We see water, as we suppose, solidifying into stones and earth, and again dissolving and evaporating into wind and air; air by combustion becomes fire. And fire in turn when extinguished and condensed takes the form of air again; air contracts and condenses into cloud and mist, and these when still more closely compacted become running water, which again turns into earth and stones. There is in fact a process of cyclical transformation.[9]

As we well know, Aristotle had also subscribed to the doctrine of four elements, and firmly believed that their structure is subject to change.

Vitruvius—an unquestionable authority throughout the Middle Ages and among the most often quoted authors of antiquity—paid due respect to earlier Greek thinkers who considered water to be the primary element. However, in his treatise on architecture Vitruvius did not dwell on philosophical premises of the world's structure, obviously taking the reflections of his predecessors on the subject for granted. He noted the biological need for water among living organisms: without getting a certain amount of water, all animals would become bloodless and perish. In the preface to book eight, referring to esoteric sources preceding those of classical Greece, Vitruvius wrote:

> Hence, too, those who are clothed in priesthoods of Egyptian orders declare that all things depend upon the power of the liquid element. So, when the waterpot is brought back to precinct and temple with water, in accordance with the holy rite, they throw

8. Aristotle, *Works*, 502.
9. Plato, *Timaeus and Critias*, 80–81.

> themselves upon the ground and, raising their hands to heaven, thank the divine benevolence for its invention. Therefore, since it is held by physicists and philosophers and priests that all things depend upon the power of water, I have thought that, as in the former seven books the rules of the buildings have been set forth, in this I ought to write on the methods of finding water ... For it is the chief requisite for life, for happiness, and for everyday use.[10]

Vitruvius provided ample practical advice on where and how water can be detected in nature, even it is not visible or its sources are hidden deep in the ground. If a man is looking for open sources, he should go out in nature, lie on the ground, and with his chest placed on the earth look around attentively at where the vapor rises. A site where there is vapor in the air is a clear sign that there is water in the area.[11] He also suggested that the qualities of the soil should be carefully examined and plants that extract humidity from the earth should be watched attentively. In many cases, however, he recommended taking special measures: using a bronze or quicksilver vessel, and after covering its interior with oil, place it bottom up on a hole five feet long and three feet wide, and put hay or greenery and earth on it. The vessel should stay in this position for at least a day. The next morning one should check whether its interior has been covered with dew. If so, this is a sign that the area contains some source of water. Vitruvius suggests another method as well—to use a vessel made of unbaked clay. Other means for detecting water were suggested as well. Vitruvius' recommendations indicate that he had a good knowledge of the geographical setting of water supplies: he advised looking for water in the mountains and areas with a northern exposure, for the quality of water is much better in them; the valleys in between mountains are also good places for finding water.[12] Some of his remarks might seem somewhat naïve, but he did all his best to provide his readers with an understanding of how water turns into vapor. For example, he writes:

> That vapour, mists, and humidity come forth from the earth, seems due to the reason that it contains burning heat, mighty currents of air, intense cold, and a great quantity of water. So, as soon as the earth, which has cooled off during the night, is struck

10. Vitruvius, *Ten Books on Architecture*, 226.
11. Ibid., 227.
12. Ibid., 228–29.

by the rays of the rising sun, and the winds begin to blow while it is yet dark, mists begin to rise upward from damp places. That the air when thoroughly heated by the sun can make vapours rise rolling up from the earth, may be seen by means of an example drawn from the baths. . . . For the earth gives out moisture under the influence of heat just as a man's heated body emits sweat.[13]

Vitruvius also warned that there are some kinds of water that are deadly dangerous to a human being. He indicates sources and territories where, because of some hazardous qualities, water is so dangerous that it is not possible to either drink it or bathe in it. At the end of his discussion of water, the author explains that some of the things mentioned in the book he presented following the insights of Greek thinkers and medical authorities, while others were discovered by him alone. This adds a certain additional value to his writings, insofar as it allows the conclusion that the Roman theorist of architecture was making his own observations and, possibly, experiments. His book contains insights into extracting and supplying water through pipe systems; he warns that lead pipes might be extremely hazardous to the health. According to Vitruvius, in many cases clay pipes are far better than those of lead, since they surpass the latter both in their construction and quality of water. This treatise of an architect contains its author's findings, but it is also a valuable source on the achievements of Roman engineering in the field of water supply. Vitruvius' recommendations were followed by later Roman art theorists. For example, in the third century Cetius Faventinus, wrote that there are four ways of supplying water, including the enclosure of bricks, lead pipes, water channels, and clay pipes. When water is supplied with the help of brick enclosures, the bricks have to be glued together so no water leakage is possible, while the canal in the middle of aqueduct should be erected following the direction of running water. When there is flat land around, the structure should be built below the water source; if the plain is wide, it should be lowered a foot and a half at the distance of every one hundred and sixty feet. These devices will give life to the stream and will provide more speed to the running water. As Vitruvius did earlier, Cetius Faventinus emphasized the danger of using lead pipe systems.[14]

For a long time in the history of civilization, as humans were forced to rely on the grace of nature, communities established their settlements

13. Ibid., 230.
14. Plommer, *Vitruvius and Later Roman Building Manuals*, 51–53.

in areas where there was an abundance of water and food. Many early cities were founded close to larger water bodies; later humans discovered and learned to develop systems of water supply. The old historical cities were, as a rule, rather small and compact: this was conditioned by military considerations, as well of those of social interaction, and last but not least—the water supply. Plato in his *Republic* claimed that the ideal city should be of such a size as to allow each citizen in any place of the city to hear the sounds of a drum urging citizens to rally in the agora. Jack Bowyer in his *History of Building* notes that the two main problems of a human being who ceased to be a nomadic being and settled permanently is to supply himself with water and to get rid of waste. Many contemporary primitive cultures used ceramic vessels for getting water from a stream or lake, relying on the power of human muscles exclusively. It was, however, discovered early in human history that after extracting water from some body of water, it is possible, by using the power of gravity, to get it moved with the help of open channels. In order to avoid leakage, canals were eventually covered with waterproof material, and in those areas where some danger occurred to the water, the canals were closed.[15]

The first channels of water supply in human history were found in the territory of ancient Persia. The peculiarities of climate (large desert areas, the lack of natural water bodies, etc.) spurred the inhabitants of Persia to develop artificial systems of water supply. In the oases of the deserts where natural bodies of water existed, gardening was the main occupation throughout the centuries. There were several types of gardens in these oases: in some of them, the water was supplied by wells, in others, channels were dug for this purpose, while in certain places the different ground level of water bodies was used. The technology of extracting water in Persian wells was rather simple—they used the power of mules and donkeys. The ancient Persians knew how to devise underground tunnels-wells, which were called *qanat*. A system already existed in 500 B.C., and was used to supply water to the city of Persepolis. Since water resources were scarce, each and every drop of water was of utmost value. It can be added that these traditional means of water supply are used in rural areas in the territory of former Persia to this very day.[16]

No matter how keenly Persians were absorbed in securing adequate water supply, no one ever surpassed the technological devices

15. Bowyer, *History of Building*, 213.
16. Crowe and Haywood, *The Gardens of Mughul India*, 30–31.

constructed by the Romans, who, as we know, were exceptionally skillful in the areas of building and engineering. Having inherited certain building practices from the Etruscans—a mysterious race that inhabited the Italian peninsula before them—the Romans further developed systems of engineering, including those of water supply, drainage, and sewerage. One should not, however, forget that other civilizations were also endowed with technological prowess. Open canals were the most widespread system almost everywhere up until the nineteenth century, but inhabitants of Crete used ceramic pipes for supplying water as early as the third century B.C. Devices of this kind found in Palestine dating from the thirteen century B.C. are known to have been much more advanced. The pipe systems of Roman times resemble drainage systems of the modern era. The pipes were made not only out of baked clay, but from metal as well. Metal pipes for water supply installed in 2500 B.C. have been found in Egypt.[17] It should be added though, that Egyptian gardeners were more willing than their Persian counterparts to rely on the power of human muscles—the reservoirs providing water for the greenery of the Egyptian gardens were serviced by slaves.[18] One of the greatest innovations in the engineering of water supply and disposal of waste was introduced in ancient Rome. Despite the fact that the "eternal city" had mostly supplied water with the help of wells, eventually canals were used for the purpose. It is noted that the Romans devised a special system for the disposal of human waste. In his monumental study of cities, Lewis Mumford has emphasized the grandeur of Rome's sewerage. As Mumford eloquently and insightfully put it:

> It is no accident that the oldest monument of Roman engineering is the Cloaca Maxima, the great sewer, constructed in the sixth century on a scale so gigantic that either its builders have clairvoyantly seen, at the earliest moment, that this heap of villages would become a metropolis of a million inhabitants, or else they must have taken for granted that the chief business and ultimate end of life is the physiological process of evacuation. So sound was the stone construction, so ample the dimensions, that this sewer is in use today. With its record of continuous service for more than twenty-five hundred years, that structure proves that in the planning of cities low first cost does not necessarily denote economy; for if the utility needed has been soundly conceived

17. Bowyer, *History of Building*, 214.
18. Berral, *The Garden*, 12–13.

and built, the final costs, extended over its whole prospective lifetime, are what really matter. On these terms, the Cloaca Maxima has turned out to be one of the cheapest pieces of engineering on record, though it is rivaled by some of the latter viaducts and bridges that are still in use, not least by the magnificent Pont du Gard in Provence.[19]

Although it might be argued that from the point of view of aesthetics that Greek cities, with their abundance of works of art in public places, surpassed Roman ones, there is no doubt that if engineering is taken as a point of departure, Roman cities were far superior. Among the greatest achievements of Roman urban culture, the baths—huge and spacious buildings constructed for leisure activities and amusement—ought to be mentioned. These cultural institutions, in which Roman citizens were not only bathing, but submerging into other bodily pleasures as well as intellectual discussions, are a testimony to Rome's unique culture of water. Drawing on the data provided by the first inventory of Rome, compiled in the year 312–315, Mumford mentions as many as 11 public baths (*thermae* in Latin). In addition, the urban space of the capital of the Roman empire contained 19 canals, 700 public basins, and 500 fountains supplied with water from 130 reservoirs.[20] Even these naked figures indicate that water was an important part of Rome's public life, and not only satisfied elementary needs but was a source of enduring bodily and spiritual joys. Aquae Sulis in the British isles was perhaps the largest complex of baths in Europe. Despite the fact that only the main bath, encircled with a row of columns of extremely perfect proportions, survives to our day, there is some evidence to believe that there were three water pools provided with water endowed with healing qualities from a very deep natural well. Researchers of this ancient monument maintain that rheumatic illnesses were treated there.[21]

The Hadrian villa in the vicinity of Tivoli is one of the most impressive surviving examples of Roman water culture. The space and architecture of the complex was united by water flowing in canals and cascades to huge basins and smaller reservoirs, fountains, and grottos, reaching each and every corner and providing musicality to a stone building.[22]

19. Mumford, *The City in History*, 214–15.
20. Ibid., 236.
21. Richmond, *Roman Britain*, 92–93.
22. Masson, *Italian Gardens*, 28.

The "Sea Theater" constructed in the building was an especially remarkable part of the whole arrangement. This was a small garden (Emperor Hadrian is known to have bathed there) with a water basin and a portico in the form of a circle. The engineering system of this villa was especially complex and refined. The water supply was provided via special cisterns to each part of the villa according to its needs. There were a number of fountains of various forms and shapes, grottos, basins, and moisturizing systems, and the used water was pumped out with the help of specially constructed underground canals.[23] Many architects of the Renaissance were deeply impressed by the aesthetics of this renowned Roman edifice, and made it a source of inspiration for their own architectural buildings. Pliny Junior provided his own account of how Romans realized the role of flowing water in architectural space. In a letter to his friend dated 62 A.D., he wrote that the water flowing from several pipes of a modest size from underneath a bench under pressure, as if it were pressed by people who sit on it, runs to a sunken stone cistern and then enters a beautiful marble basin whose volume was measured with such accuracy that it always remained full, but water never rose so high as to pour out. Renowned nineteenth century French architectural theorist Viollet-le-Duc was fascinated by the construction of Roman baths. In his lectures on architecture he emphasized the number of rooms of different purposes that existed in Roman baths: among them there was the main building, water reservoirs, the lobby, wardrobes, rooms for redressing and oil procedures before entering hot and cold water basins, and training and discussion halls.[24]

After the Roman empire disintegrated, a waning of civilization took over Europe, and many of the achievements of Roman material culture were forgotten for a long time, or were converted to other uses by the militant barbarian tribes who adapted them to their own lifestyle and understanding of comfort. For example, the Anglo-Saxons and Jutes who conquered the British Isles in the fifth century destroyed the paved roads and used the stones as building material for their own dwelling houses. Thus baths and water culture as practiced and experienced by the Romans was forgotten.

---

23. McDonald and Pinto, *Hadrian's Villa*, 170–71.
24. Viollet-le-Duc, *Lectures*, 121.

THE SYMBOLISM OF WATER

Baptism, a symbol of salvation and life's new meaning—one of the oldest and most fundamental rites of Christianity—is closely bonded to water. The meaning of water to the ritual of baptism was expressed in a treatise on symbolism of the thirteenth century, in which Durantis wrote that if a human being is not reborn again out of water and Spirit, he or she will not be able to get into the kingdom of God. Thus the role of water was not only to wash away the dirtiness of a human body but also to clean the sins of his or her soul.[25] The fountain of *The Song of Songs*, according to Christian symbologist Gerhart Ladner, is related not only to the rivers of heaven but also to symbolism of baptism and a river that cleanses.[26] In early Christianity the location of a baptism was not given great import. Since Christ himself received baptism while wading in the Jordan river, the followers of his faith could follow his example. The first Christian liturgies indicate that the Christian Church had no inclination to limit the place of the procedure very strictly. A book from the year 120 A.D. entitled *The Teaching of Twelve Apostles* only said that this ritual of utmost importance should be performed in running water; however, in a case where it is not available, any other body of water— either cold or hot—can be used. Regardless, the one who baptizes pours water on the head of the baptized three times in the name of God the Father, the Son of God, and the Holy Spirit.[27] In drawings found in the catacombs of early Christians, a man is depicted as standing in water up to his ankles, and the baptist is shown with an arm stretched over his head. There were no regulations, either about what season or in which particular place the baptism should take place. The texts of the apostles testify that baptism took place in various places such as private homes and roadsides, but eventually the rules became tighter.[28] The fact that this rite was performed in such a liberal way might be explained by the dangers that threatened early adherents of this cult. Persecuted and punished, spied on and betrayed, they took precautions to practice their rituals in secret; thus baptism took place in places that were more or less safe, mostly in the private homes of people who had already become

---

25. Durantis, *The Symbolism of Church*, 117.
26. Ladner, *God, Cosmos, and Humankind*, 143.
27. Milburn, *Early Christian Art*, 203.
28. Bond, *Fonts and Font Covers*, 24.

Christians. With the passing of time, the practice changed, and when Christianity became firmly established, bishops issued orders to install special small buildings close to the churches for fonts. It is recorded that the bishop Paulinus, while building his cathedral in Trier in the year 314, erected several buildings attached to the basilica for this purpose.[29] The first fonts were usually built in a circular form with a cross-shaped basin in the middle, but there were fonts of other configurations, especially octagonal. The number eight had a special symbolic meaning: since God created the world in six days and took a rest on the seventh, the eighth day represented hope associated with the resurrection of Christ.[30] The symbolism of the number eight, which meant the death of Christ and his resurrection (Easter), also signified Sunday and eternity.[31] Water was supplied to fonts with the help of pipes produced out of lead or clay, but some fonts were filled with the help of dippers. Some fonts were very small, with room for just one person; others were large enough to accommodate eight individuals at a time. Luxurious fonts were constructed in later periods. One such splendid font was created by order of Sixtus the III on Lateran Hill in the year 435. Although it was reconstructed several times, as one can judge from engravings made in the sixteenth century, its original classic form was maintained. The interior space of the font is divided into two octagons by eight columns, which have most probably survived since the times of Constantine. The original basin of the font with life-sized sculptures of Jesus Christ and John the Baptist was destroyed, but the theology of baptism is expressed by the verses engraved around the architrave.

Water was especially venerated in the East. In the culture of Islam, water is the symbol of divine cognition and knowledge. Water contained in fountains was used during Muslim rituals to wash the hands and feet before entering the mosque for prayer. Since ancient times, pipelines of fanciful configurations were an important decorative element, and the water that streamed through them into the basins of interior spaces in palaces was used for pleasure and recreation. Moorish Alhambra was especially famous for its water effects—to this very day it is considered to be one of the most perfect and breathtaking examples of the Islamic culture of water. Various water bodies performed different functions in

29. Milburn, *Early Christian Art*, 204.
30. Ibid., 206.
31. Ladner, *God, Cosmos, and Humankind*, 248.

Alhambra: some were designated for repose and relaxation, others provided shelter from heat during the day. Last but not least, they provided enormous aesthetic pleasure. The middle fountain was perfectly staged to fit the description of the heavens and the four rivers running beneath them in the Koran. The canals of Alhambra, arranged according to the traditions of Byzantine and Persian gardens, were constantly filled with water so that human eyes could derive pleasure from the mirror-like shining of their surface. Canals were also used for fulfilling the needs of drainage and cooling, although water was supplied to the main fountain with the help of pipes. Canals crossing the Lions' Yard contain bonds to an even older tradition—to the times when pipelines were not yet invented and water was supplied in an open manner. Canals were situated according in almost the same plan in the mosque of Samara, dating from the ninth century, as well as Balcuvara's gardens in Mesopotamia.[32]

During the Christian Middle Ages, metaphysical meaning was given not only to baptism but to water as a substance. When building edifices, medieval people used to ascribe a particular meaning to each building material they used in the process. Henry Taylor, researcher into medieval ways of thinking, emphasizes that the mortar to glue bricks together was produced out of lime, sand, and water. The medieval mind interpreted lime as a passionate love that helps to attract sand, which was understood as earthly labor, while water was treated as a spirit that brings lime and sand together. Thus, in the same way as stone walls cannot be stable without mortar, people cannot hope to enter heavenly Jerusalem without the love provided by the Holy Spirit.[33] In this mode of thought water was treated symbolically and metaphysically. Among Christian communities there was a widespread notion in which water was compared to the Holy Church. Testimonies of this kind are found in the sermons of St. Ambrose, who said that the sea is often compared to the Church, in which, as soon as people congregate, a "tide starts," and later when they are united in prayer the church is filled with rustle as if the waves were moving away. Moreover, the voices of men, women, and children chanting psalms was reminiscent of the sound of breaking waves. St. Ambrose also reminded his listeners that water cleans away sin when the Holy Spirit is breathing over it in the name of salvation.[34]

32. Bargebuhr, *Alhambra*, 179.
33. Taylor, *The Medieval Mind*, 105.
34. Paredi, *Saint Ambrose*, 269.

THE CULTURE OF WATER IN THE MIDDLE AGES, RENAISSANCE, AND BAROQUE

Medieval urban dwellers supplied themselves with water from wells that were dug in the cities. Wells in the vicinity of large towns were used as well. The organized supply of water in London dates to the year 1237. Common ordinary city dwellers and public fountains were supplied by pipelines scraped from the trunks of elm, while the upper levels of society hired special carriers to bring water to their places of residence. The surplus water was directed to canals and basins where men and women bathed together.[35] Romans used to construct their wells from oak trees, while during the medieval period in Britain brick wells were usually used.[36] Town dwellers used to throw waste straight into the streets, and consequently medieval towns were exposed to unsanitary conditions; the plague or "black death" was a constant reality throughout that period. Somewhat better conditions were created in monasteries, where used water was poured into special vessels to wash away the dirt. The fact that medieval towns suffered from a lack of sanitation should not mislead us into thinking that no hygiene was observed during the Middle Ages. Places for bathing dug up in Southern Italy dating to the thirteenth century are a testimony that bathing was a common practice in that period of human history. The plan for the Abbey of Saint Gall, containing special bath nooks for the abbot, monks, and novices, supports this idea. It is known that in the town of Salerno the nuns were not allowed to use public baths, and the monastery of Cluny contained a special bathroom for intimate procedures.[37]

Water regained its aesthetic importance in the Renaissance. When the fashion of maintaining suburban villas in the vicinity of Rome came into being, gardening and the establishing of parks became a usual practice. Wealthy owners of these villas aimed to create a balance between nature and architecture: beautiful and carefully proportioned edifices were surrounded by spectacular and carefully developed gardens. Water "fireworks" were frequently arranged for recreational purposes in the gardens of the advanced European countries of the period. Water would

---

35. Berral, *The Garden*, 95.
36. Bowyer, *History of Building*, 216.
37. Caskey, "Steam and 'Sanitas'," 170.

usually erupt from an opening hidden in the earth and splash the astonished and delighted visitors, who were keenly interested in this type of amusement.[38] Water became a natural source of beauty that created an exclusive atmosphere and hypnotized visitors with a multitude of visual and acoustic effects. Following the example of Roman villas, Italian architects sought symbiotic relations between the natural environment and architectural forms. As landscape historian John Simonds has emphasized, many of these villas produced and continue to produce their impression because of their "symphonic beauty," especially since the designers of these landscape compositions were extremely fond of local topography, greenery, plants, and water. He notes that we can hardly find any other place where water as an element of landscape was used with more imagination than in Villa d'Este, and where water and other elements of nature were combined so as to produce the most perfect combinations of these elements.[39] Georgina Masson, researcher of Renaissance gardens, claims that this beautiful work of architecture was considered one of the most impressive architectural compositions in Italy for a number of centuries, though shifting according to the aesthetic principles of each epoch. She notes that when Michael de Montaigne, renowned French philosopher and essayist, visited this place sometime around 1580 or 1581, neither the edifice nor the garden were completed, and yet the insight peculiar to the French aesthete enabled him to realize that the impressive system of water distribution installed in the rooms of the lower floor was modeled according to unsurpassed Roman examples. He was especially astonished by the abundance of water and the fountains around the basins containing fish: the spray of the water glistened in the air and created rainbows.[40]

Many other carefully designed and perfectly decorated Renaissance suburban residences other than Villa d'Este were famous for their water effects, including the beautiful Villa Lante, designed by the architect Vignola for Cardinal Gambara; Villa Barbaro, designed strictly following Roman architectural examples by Andrea Palladio; and the garden island of Boboli—the most famous among the gardens of Medici dynasty—which the artist, architect, and biographer Giorgio Vasari claimed was the creation of his friend Tribolo. While designing these famous gardens

38. Briggs, *The Architect in History*, 156.
39. Simonds, *Landscape Architecture*, 72.
40. Masson, *Italian Gardens*, 156.

and residences, Italian architects followed the example of the villa of the Roman emperor Hadrian (who lived in the first century), and put in a lot of effort to make sure all the water bodies were used to the utmost. It might be justly said that in no other period of European history was such a perfect balance and harmony between architecture and its natural surrounding established than in the Roman tradition of the Italian *Rinascimento*.[41] The American writer Edith Wharton, who visited Italy in the year 1900, was captivated by the perfect beauty of Italian gardens. She documented her impression in an insightful study of the garden design and architecture of villas. While focusing on aesthetic qualities of Villa Lante, she wrote that the design of the flower garden is beautiful and complex—there is an abundance of flowers around one of the most famous and beautiful fountains in Italy. The abundance of water in its own way allowed the architect to create a multitude of effects called "water art" by Germans.[42] The villas of the Frascati region were also famous for their water aesthetics. The first suburban residences in Frascati were built during Roman times by wealthy town dwellers, who sought relief from the summer heat in the surroundings of nature. The Italian Renaissance philosopher and philologist Annibale Caro, closely following Roman traditions, built Villa Torlonia on the mountain slope over Frascati, and found two more residences in the neighborhood belonging to cardinals Alessandro Ruffino and Montepulciano. Shortly afterwards another architectural edifice—Villa Aldobrandini—was built in the vicinity, where, according to Carl L. Frank, the acoustic qualities of water were especially emphasized: side by side with visual effects, sound effects were produced with the help of water organs.[43] Streams of running water were directed to wind instruments, and produced various sounds, from the horn of centaur to the subtle murmur of water on the hill, or hissing as it came through the threatening jaws of a stone tiger. People travelled long distances to experience the pleasures of the sounds and undergo a "wet surprise"—water engineers had constructed an abundance of them all over the territory of the villa.[44] The architectural design was created by the architect Giacomo della Porta, implemented by Maderna, while

---

41. Eckbo, *Landscape We See*, 94.
42. Wharton, *Italian Villas and Their Gardens*, 135.
43. Franck, *Villas of Frascati*, 8–9.
44. Ibid., 28.

the hydraulic construction was produced by Orazio Olivieri, the engineer of the famous water systems of Villa d'Este.[45]

Engineering principles of water supply were thoroughly discussed in the treatises of Renaissance architectural theory. In his tenth book on architecture, Leon Battista Alberti wrote that when a suitable source of water is found, one needs to take care of how to supply it. And for this purpose there are two methods: direct it with the help of a canal or establish a pipeline. The builder, however, has to beware that the place where the water has to be supplied isn't higher than its source—in this case special measures must be taken. Water running through a canal should be directed downwards all the way, but when it runs through the pipeline in some place it should be directed upwards.[46]

The aesthetics of landscape and park architecture continued to be of importance in the Baroque era as well. Water bodies were assigned a special visual and recreational importance when the European nobility, following the example of the French king Louis XIV, started to erect suburban residencies in refined landscape settings, and court life moved to luxurious, spacious suburban residences that provided ample settings for various kinds of pleasures. The architect Le Notre, who was commissioned to design the parks of Versailles, assigned an exclusive importance to the optical effects of water surfaces. With fountains and "mirrors of sleeping water" placed among precisely shaped geometrical tree paths and greenery of meadows, he create a landscape that perfectly reflected the ambitions of the epoch of absolutism.[47] The water cascade "Obelisk" was constructed in one of the gardens of the park, called Salle du Conseil. Water jets were laid out to create the shape of an obelisk, and the streams of water were so strong that the falling water became as white as snow. This complicated installation, however, did not survive to the present day, but an image of it can be recreated with the help of drawings and engravings of the period.[48] Another water body of Versailles, the fountain of Latona, was full of ambiguous metaphors as well as more direct mythological allusions. As architectural historian Vincent Scully has noted, the ballet in the fountain of Latona starts as soon as the water starts streaming from the mouths of the miserable peasants who con-

45. Ibid., 124.
46. Alberti, *On the Art of Building*, 221.
47. Bazin, *Baroque and Rococo*, 124.
48. Triggs, *Garden Craft in Europe*, 103.

demned Latona and her son, and were sentenced by Zeus to become frogs and lizards. However, these figures actually represent the citizens of Paris who insulted Louis XIV and his mother during the Fronde riots. Moreover, four parts of iconography can be found in Latona, and Louis, according to Scully's interpretation, becomes earth, air, fire, and water.[49]

No matter what effects were created in Versailles, the Italians remained unsurpassed in the sphere of water and landscape architecture, providing a multitude of visual effects in their gardens and parks. As Tassilo Wengel has remarked, even the smallest and most insignificant Italian garden contains a soothing source of water, and he considers that the aesthetic formation of water bodies was turned by Italians into an art that changed the whole visual image of gardens.[50] And yet no matter how resourcefully water bodies such as basins and fountains were designed, the era of the aesthetics of water in France, except perhaps in places like Versailles, was soon over. The testimony of water's importance to the landscape was documented by the Marquis de Girarden, who wrote of the philosophical role of water in a landscape. The Marquis maintained that water in a landscape is the same as eyes in the face of a human being; they are capable of rousing great emotions when they are wide and deep, and they let such feelings as fear surface when they are foaming or turbid. He was convinced that there is not a single emotion that cannot be provoked, sustained, or soothed with the help of water.[51]

WATER CULTURE IN MODERN URBANISM

The philosopher Arthur Schopenhauer, discussing the place of architecture in his hierarchy of the arts, insisted that aesthetic character is not the most essential goal in the art of architecture, because it always strives for utility and performs practical functions. Because of this specific quality, he treated architecture as lower than other kinds of art—sculpture, painting, poetry or music—to which he gave the highest aesthetic importance, considering their ability to appeal to the human soul without any mediation. Since Schopenhauer, music is usually considered the highest among all the arts, the art that all the others are compared to. Higher than architecture in his division of arts was the architecture of

---

49. Scully, *Architecture*, 228–29.
50. Wengel, *Art of Gardening*, 78.
51. Baltrušaitis, *Aberrations*, 175.

cascades, ponds, and fountains, along with parks and gardens, as they are not subordinate to any kind of utility. Waterfalls that run down from rocks, fountains that rise up as if they were columns, and the clear waters of lakes all reveal the idea of liquid hard material, as works of architecture reveal the idea of frozen material, Schopenhauer claimed.[52]

Despite Schopenhauer's favorable attitude toward the aesthetic arrangement of water as a specific and independent art form exceeding the aesthetic qualities of architecture, his philosophical insight into this problem had little relation to developments in real life, especially in a Western culture that was being shaped by a new urban context. The Industrial Revolution, which gave technological impetus to the development of Western culture, resulted in cities being taken hostage. With the rise of industrialism and modern urbanism, the role of water in cities and large towns was gradually reduced to the level of practical utilitarian needs, except perhaps those tiny areas where water served for recreational leisure purposes.

In later times, despite of, or because of, rapid urban development, sanitary conditions in Western cities were poor. Waste was usually thrown away into the rivers; organized municipal disposal of waste had not yet come into being. Even as late as the nineteenth century, large European urban metropolises such as London suffered from a lack of adequate sanitation. In this sense London is symptomatic example that helps us to understand the situation of other European cities. There was no sewerage in London: the entire sewage system was made of pipes that let down dirty water to the nearest water reservoir, most often into Thames River. One can understand why, according to Lewis Mumford, pigs were kept in central areas of London in order to deal with waste up until the mid-nineteenth century. No wonder thinkers and utopian urban planners of the period focused on the cleanliness and hygiene of urban spaces as one of the most essential conditions of human health. Hygiene and cleanliness became important elements in the life of the imagined communities of the future. Such shifts in the paradigms of thinking were reflected, for example, in certain Swedish periodicals, whose main topic were issues of social hygiene. One doctor of medicine named Grahs published an educational article about health care, which claimed that there are three main values and conditions for good health: air, water, and light. A book by Niels Eglund about the uses of bathing

52. Schopenhauer, *Pasaulis*, 314.

and skin care was published in Sweden in the year 1887. As time went on, the culture of bathing enveloped not only discourses of hygiene, but also those of ethics and aesthetics.[53] These intellectual initiatives in Sweden contributed greatly to the development of baths among the population.

Many historical cities were established close to the larger reservoirs of water. The junctions of rivers and sea and the banks of large rivers and lakes were chosen because of their military advantages and long-distance communication opportunities. A large water reservoir not only contributed to a city's defense potential, but was also a source of usable water during periods of siege. In the ancient times as well as in the life of traditional communities, a well or spring performed the functions of a village center. Marshall McLuhan has provided evidence that in some areas, these functions are being performed to this very day: when the United Nations implemented a program of centralized water supply in some Indian villages, a few months later representatives of a village approached the local administration with a request to disassemble the pipeline. The request was motivated by the explanation that after the pipeline was constructed, village dwellers no longer had the need to gather at the local well for water and at the same time to talk about matters concerning the daily life of their community: the well had served as informal community center before the establishment of the pipeline.

Water became the target of progressive engineers in the modern epoch, when progress ideology became the essential driving force in understanding the relationship between human beings and nature. Attacking Austrian architect Camillo Sitte, who was captivated by the beauty of the aesthetics of medieval cities and urged urban planners to reconsider their approach toward the legacy of the past, Le Corbusier—one of the most influential architects and urban thinkers of the last century—urged city planners to disregard the urban legacy. He was convinced that progress in urban development can only be based on two strategies: therapy and surgery. Summing up the situation of modern cities, Le Corbusier wrote: "The great capitals have no arteries; they have only capillaries: further growth, therefore, implies sickness or death. In order to survive, their existence has for a long time been in the hands of surgeons who operate constantly."[54] Le Corbusier observed of modern urban planning that nature develops in a chaotic way, and the task of a human being is to

---

53. Nillson, "The Need," 206.
54. Le Corbusier, *City of To-morrow*, 25.

give it strict forms based on geometry and mathematics. No wonder he praised the Romans for the invention of a square plan for city building, as well as for the regularity and orderliness of their cities. Le Corbusier preached city building based on the principle of *tabula rasa*—i.e., first cleaning the sites of historical cities, and then building everything from scratch so as to give the urban planner full potential for developing his vision of the city of tomorrow. Lakes and rivers had no place in his vision of contemporary urbanity. In his seminal book *The City of To-morrow and Its Planning*, Le Corbusier insisted that "The river flows far away from the city. The river is a kind of liquid railway, a goods station and a sorting house. In a decent house the servant's stairs do not go through the drawing-room—even if the maid is charming (or if the little boats delight the loiterer leaning on a bridge)."[55] This strict, rigid, uncompromising statement demonstrates Le Corbusier's dismissal of the aesthetic qualities of water bodies in cities. To an architect who was thinking and acting in terms of mechanistic philosophy and in the name of so-called progress, water was no more than an element of modern engineering. If Sitte argued in favor of the irregular beauty of medieval towns and urged architects to preserve the twisting streets and natural topography for which medieval European cities were famous, his opponent hailed strict geometry, logic, and order. There was no place for a lake, river, or pond in Le Corbusier's vision of ordered modern city life.

The ideology preached by Le Corbusier had a huge impact on several generations of future architects and urban planners, who chose to disregard the legacy of the past and set out to follow the path determined by the powerful ideology of urban progress. By following neo-functionalist doctrines and principles of modern aesthetics and city building, Corbusier's successors neglected the aesthetic aspect of water bodies in the urban environment, or designed urban spaces so that those "servant's stairs" should remain isolated from the "façade" of a modern city, or planned to envelop rivers in concrete as if they were "liquid railroads."

However, it should be taken into consideration that this understanding of water's role in contemporary urban design had powerful opponents as well. Frank Lloyd Wright, one of the leading architects of the last century, who was endowed with powerful vision and deep insight into the legacies of different cultures, was especially sensitive to natural forms and natural landscape. Frank Lloyd Wright contributed

55. Ibid., 173.

to a completely different understanding of modern architecture in an urban setting, offering an architectural vision in which the symbiosis between nature and architecture was strongly emphasized. His famous concept of "organic architecture" reflects a deep understanding of nature and natural beauty, the wisdom of ancient builders, and the architectural traditions of the East. Wright's architecture undoubtedly bears resemblance to the principles embedded in the traditional architecture of Eastern cultures, mainly Buddhism, especially the respect for nature inherent in it. Parallels between Wright's architectural works and the Oriental way of building have been visible in his architecture since his "Prairie School period," where horizontal lines predominate, as they do in the traditional edifices of Asian architecture. I choose to use the word parallels instead of influences, since Frank Lloyd Wright himself has admitted that what is considered Oriental in his art he had discovered before he was acquainted with Eastern philosophy and architecture. As Clay Lancaster noted in his discussion of the architectural principles of the Far East:

> From Occidental and Oriental viewpoints regarding the individual comes the fifth principle, the distinction of verticality in the West as opposed to horizontality in the Far East. The upright line represents the rugged individualist, discrete and unswerving; the horizontal line of repose typifies him who is attuned to the universe, who sees himself mirrored in all things and all things in him—the contour of sea that embraces the nonillion drops of water in a single ocean.[56]

One of the remarkable pieces of Wright's architectural genius, Fallingwater, is an example of perfect symbiosis between nature and architecture. Henry Russell Hitchcock has justly called it "one of the first and most striking demonstrations that a new cycle of world architecture had opened, a cycle, alas, destined within two or three years for a premature end in Europe with a coming of war."[57]

Frank Lloyd Wright was extremely conscious of the underlined contrast and interaction between the hardness of stone and the fluidity of water. He himself gave an explanation of his treatment of water while presenting Fallingwater in 1938. Wright emphasized that:

---

56. Lancaster, "Metaphysical Beliefs," 297.
57. Hitchcock, *In the Nature of Materials*, 91–92.

This building is a late example of the inspiration of a site, the cooperation of an intelligent, appreciative client and the use of entirely masonry materials except for an interlining of redwood and asphalt beneath all flooring. Again, by the way of steel in tension this building takes its place and achieves its form. The grammar of the slabs at their eaves is best shown by a detail. But the roof water is caught by a lead string built into the concrete above near the beginning of the curve... it is not the deluge of water in a storm that hurts any building: it is ooze and drip of dirty water in thawing and freezing, increased by slight showers. . . . This structure might serve to indicate that the sense of shelter—the sense of space where used with sound structural sense—has no limitations as to form except the materials used and the methods by which they are employed for what purpose.[58]

English art historian and critic Adrian Stokes, who investigated the heritage of the Italian Quattrocento in Rimini, recorded his impressions while observing the peculiar relationship between stone bas-reliefs and water: "And of those feelings of which I write throughout these volumes, I consider the most fundamental one to be connected with the interaction of stone and water. In a sense, the fecund stone-blossom is already connected with some association of moisture in the stone."[59] Although Stokes brought his reader's attention to the specific qualities of stone relief and stressed that marble expresses its primary power of life in water, he nevertheless felt that interactions between stone and water are most clearly represented in architecture. Japanese architect Tadao Ando, who designed the impressive sanctuary Hompuku-ji, has demonstrated that the relationship between a hard material and the mirror-like surface of water is capable of creating metaphysical sensations that urge meditation and prayer. A completely different piece of architecture—the Piazza d'Italia designed by Charles Moore in New Orleans—demonstrates the architect's fantasy and sense of humor while using water in architectural spaces. Colorful materials that differ from their classical antecedents transform the stylistics in a postmodern way, while the water surface covering the mosaic of the basin enabled the architect to create a playful and ironic atmosphere—a witty reply to the great Italian epoch of art and architecture. The Groningen museum in the Netherlands, designed by Alessandro Mendini and his team (1990–1994), represents a conscious

58. Wright, *Writings and Buildings*, 272–76.
59. Stokes, *The Image in Form*, 50.

interpretation of architecture and water. The edifice of the museum, somewhat reminiscent of an Egyptian temple, stands on the bank of a canal, and thus visitors encounter a mirror reflection of the building in water before entering it. A body of water envelopes the Rock and Roll Hall of Fame in Cleveland and creates a neutral environment for the precise geometrical forms of the main building as if it were emerging from the depth of water (architect I. M. Pei). These few examples indicate that some contemporary architects are extremely conscious of the role of water in the environment of architecture, no matter whether it is an urban setting or the exterior or interior of a particular building. The hardness of architectural material and the blissful effects of water provide a plentitude of opportunities for big and small sensual aesthetic pleasures.

In a thoughtful essay "H2O and the Waters of Forgetfulness" Ivan Illich, a philosopher and historian medievalist following the path taken by his predecessor the French thinker Gaston Bachelard, has brilliantly demonstrated why the understanding of the archetypal powers of water has changed with the course of Western civilization, and why water, which the ancient Greeks associated with dreams, was finally degraded to an elementary liquid, a mechanical substance for washing away human urban waste. As Illich argued, dreams provide catharsis, or in other words, they are capable of cleaning. The water of dreams can clean in several ways: sprinkling with sanctified water disperses miasmas, removes curses, washes away dirt, and, when it is being poured on hands, head, or feet, can clean dirt, blood, and fault.[60] Water is also related to catharsis, because those who entered the kingdom of the dead and crossed the waters of mythological river Lethe were freed from their reminiscences and memory returned back to where it belongs—to the earth. This metaphorical understanding of the power of water, however, was lost in the industrial epoch, when a mechanical understanding of nature and human society took over old mythological assumptions, which is why water in a modern city became a liquid suitable only for washing away waste. As Illich has emphasized, the nineteenth century architects of London, captivated by the discovery of British surgeon William Harvey about how blood circulates in the human body, started to imagine the city as a kind of social body, through which water must circulate constantly, carrying away the waste and dirt. Its main function was seen as washing away dirt, thus the faster the circulation, the more healthy the body of

---

60. Illich, *In the Mirror*, 146.

the city becomes. And despite the fact that water was always used for the purpose of cleansing dirt in a city, this was understood as a normal and natural component of a community's life; it was only much later, with the advent of Enlightenment, that the territory of a city was seen as a place which has a smell of evil; ergo, it must be washed constantly. This is how, according to the thinker, the utopia of a scentless city was born, and water became nothing more than a liquid for the implementation of modern social engineering.[61]

SUMMING UP

Despite mental habits shaped and structured by modernity and its ideological concepts, one can still encounter architectural designs exhibiting deviations from such powerful dogmas like those imposed by Le Corbusier and his followers, who went so far as to attempt to ban the very existence of waterways in contemporary cities, as if water was something completely alien to the modern way of urban life. Some large metropolises have realized, and more and more are realizing, that water bodies are needed in city structure not only for functional purposes, but also as a vital and never-ending source of aesthetic emotions, wellbeing, and meaningful leisure activities. No wonder that those large metropolises that have allowed themselves the "luxury" of having a sufficient number of water bodies such as rivers, lakes, ponds, etc., are considered more attractive to their citizens and visitors alike. More and more architects are taking conscious steps to make water more open to city dwellers, and to enliven the water culture of their urban milieu. For example, in the mid-nineties of the last century, the English architect Richard Rogers proposed a renovation project of the embankment of London that would make the river one of the most essential places of attraction. The embankment was interpreted by the architect as important space of communication and recreation, one that needs essential reconstruction. Rogers imagined a riverside park stretching from Parliament to Blackfriars, opening into the river where boats and pontoons and bridges with other installations would unite numerous London monuments and sights into a huge public space of previously impossible dimensions.[62] In 1994–1995, Rogers developed a concept of restructuring the southern

---

61. Ibid., 150–51.
62. Rogers, *Cities for a Small Planet*, 128–39.

side of the embankment of London, and suggested covering certain edifices of this area with a "crystal roof," which would not only give more allure to the cultural institutions and commercial enterprises located in the vicinity but would also improve the possibilities of enjoying the river throughout the year, no matter what the weather conditions. These attempts show a fresh approach toward the relations between water bodies in the city and the urban environment.

Although the urban spaces of the southern countries of the world have traditionally been more associated with water, technological advancement has provided ample possibilities for the development of what I have called "water culture." A number of cities in Scandinavian countries, where the climate is more inclement, are famous for their creative use of water in urban settings. And despite the fact that in many historical cultures water has played a much more important part in people's urban and suburban life, there is still hope that people of the "late modern" epoch might wish to reconsider the place of water in our urban futures.

Bibliography

Alberti, Leon Battista. *On the Art of Building in Ten Books.* Translated by Joseph Rykwert, Neil Leach and Robert Tavernor. Cambridge: MIT Press, 1997.

———. *On Painting and On Sculpture. The Latin texts of De pictura and De statua,* edited and translated by Cecil Grayson. London: Phaidon, 1972.

Anonymous of St. Emmeram. *De Musica Mensurata.* Translated by J. Yudkin. Bloomington: Indiana University Press, 1990.

Aquinas, Thomas. *The Summa Theologica.* Great Books of the Western World 19–20. Translated by the Fathers of the English Dominican Province. Chicago and London: Encyclopedia Britannica, 1952.

Aristotle. *The Works of Aristotle.* Great Books of the Western World 8–9. Chicago and London: Encyclopedia Britannica, 1955.

Arnheim, Rudolf. *Art and Visual Perception: A Psychology of Creative Eye.* Berkeley and Los Angeles: University of California Press, 1954.

———. *The Split and the Structure.* Berkeley, Los Angeles, and London: University of California Press, 1996.

Aubert, Marcel. *The Art of the High Gothic Era.* New York: Greystone Press, 1965.

Augustine, Saint. *The Confessions, The City of God, On Christian Doctrine.* Great Books of the Western World 18. Translated by M. Dods, et al. Chicago and London: Encyclopedia Britannica, 1955.

Aveni, Anthony. "Is Harmony at the Heart of Things?" *Wilson Quarterly* 4 (2001) 54–65.

Bagenal, Hope. *Practical Acoustics and Planning Against Noise.* New York: Chemical Publishing Company, 1942.

Baltrušaitis, Jurgis. *Aberrations: An Essay on the Legend of Forms.* Translated by Richard Miller. Cambridge: MIT Press, 1989.

Banham, Reyner. *The Architecture of the Well-Tempered Environment.* London: The Architectural Press, 1969.

Bargebuhr, Frederick. *The Alhambra: A Cycle of Studies on the Eleventh Century in Moorish Spain.* Berlin: Walter de Gruyter and Co., 1968.

Barnes, Jonathan. *The Presocratic Philosophers.* London: Routledge and Kegan Paul, 1982.

Bayley, Harold. *The Lost Language of Symbolism.* Secaucus, NJ: Citadel Press, 1988.

Bazin, Germain. *Baroque and Rococo.* London: Thames and Hudson, 1979.

Beranek, Leo L. *Music, Acoustics, and Architecture.* New York and London: John Wiley and Sons, 1962.

Berral, Julia. *The Garden: An Illustrated History.* Harmondsworth: Penguin, 1961.

Boethius. *Fundamentals of music / Anicius Manlius Severinus Boethius*. Translated by Calvin M. Bower. New Haven: Yale University Press, 1989.
——— (Boecij). "Nastavlenije k muzike." In *Istorija estetiki*, t. 1. Moskva, 1962.
Bonaventure, Saint. *Works of Saint Bonaventure*. Vol. I. Translated by E.T. Healy. New York: The Franciscan Institute, 1955.
Bond, Francis. *Fonts and Font Covers*. London: Waterstone Press, 1985.
Bosanquet, Bernard. *A History of Aesthetics*. London: George Allen and Unwin, 1917.
Bowyer, Jack. *History of Building*. London: Crosby Lockwood Staples, 1973.
Briggs, Martin S. *The Architect in History*. New York: Da Capo Press, 1974.
Bronsted, Johannes. *The Vikings*. Translated by Kalle Skov. Harmondsworth, England: Penguin, 1965.
Brown, Sarah. *Stained Glass: An Illustrated History*. London: Bracken Books, 1994.
Buivydas, Rimantas. "Simbolis ir architektūra. Ankstyvasis periodas." *Urbanistika ir architektūra* 1 (1997) 86–99.
Carritt, E. F. *Philosophies of Beauty from Socrates to Robert Bridges*. Oxford: Clarendon Press, 1931.
Caskey, Jill. "Steam and 'Sanitas' in the Domestic Realm: Baths and Bathing in Southern Italy in the Middle Ages." *Journal of the Society of Architectural Historians* 58:2 (1999) 170–95.
Cirlot, Juan Eduardo. *The Dictionary of Symbols*. London: Routledge, 1995.
Clark, Kenneth. *Civilization: A Personal View*. London: BBC and John Murray, 1969.
Clarke, Brian, ed. *Architectural Stained Glass*. New York: Architectural Record Books, 1979.
Crow, Sylvia and Sheila Haywood. *The Gardens of Mughul India: A History and Guide*. London: Thames and Hudson, 1972.
Cunningham, Lawrence L., and John J. Reich. *Culture and Values: A Survey of Western Humanities*. New York: Holt, Rinehart and Winston. 1985.
Dillistone, Frederick William. *Christianity and Symbolism*. London: SCM Press, 1985.
Durantis, Guilelmus. *The Symbolism of Church and Church Ornaments*. Translated by John Mason Neale and Benjamin Webb. New York: AMS Press, 1973.
Eckbo, Garrett. *The Landscape We See*. New York: McGraw-Hill, 1969.
Eco, Umberto. *Art and Beauty in the Middle Ages*. Translated by Hugh Bredin. New Haven: Yale University Press, 1986.
———. *Menas ir grožis viduramžių estetikoje*. Translated by Jonas Vilimas. Vilnius: Baltos lankos, 1997.
Etlin, Richard A. *Frank Lloyd Wright and Le Corbusier: the Romantic Legacy*. Manchester and New York: Manchester University Press, 1994.
Ficino, Marsilio. In *The Renaissance Philosophy of Man*, edited by Ernst Cassirer, et.al. Chicago: University of Chicago Press, 1954.
Fideler, David F., ed. *The Pythagorean Sourcebook and Library*. Compiled and translated by K. S. Guthrie, et.al. Grand Rapids: Phanes Press, 1987.
Fiske, John. *Myths and Myth-makers*. Boston and New York: Houghton Mifflin, 1900.
Fludd, Robert. *Robert Fludd and His Philosophical Key*. Introduced by A. L. Debus. New York: Science History Publications, 1979.
Foster, Michael. *The Principles of Architecture: Style, Structure and Design*. Oxford: Phaidon, 1982.
Franck, Carl Ludwig. *The Villas of Frascati: 1550–1750*. New York: Transatlantic Arts, 1966.

Frankl, Paul. *The Gothic: Literary Sources and Interpretations Through Eight Centuries*. Princeton: Princeton University Press, 1960.
Fridugis. "Letter on Nothing and Darkness." In *Medieval Philosophy: From St. Augustine to Nicholas of Cusa*, edited by J. F. Wipel and A. B. Wolter, 107–108. New York: Free Press, 1969.
Gafurio, Franchino. *The Theory of Music*. Translated by Walter Kurt Kreyszig. New Haven: Yale University Press, 1993.
Gilson, Etienne. *History of Christian Philosophy in the Middle Ages*. New York: Random House, 1955.
Gimbutienė (Gimbutas), Marija. *Senoji Europa*. Vilnius: Mokslo ir enciklopedijų leidykla, 1996.
Godwin, Joscelyn. *The Harmony of the Spheres: A Sourcebook of the Pythagorean Tradition in Music*. Rochester, VT: Inner Traditions International, 1993.
———. *Mystery Religions in the Ancient World*. San Francisco: Harper and Row, 1981.
Goethe, Johann Wolfgang von, *Goethe's Color Theory*. Translated by H. Aach. New York: Van Nostrand Reinhold, 1971.
Goldsmith, Elisabeth Edwards. *Ancient Pagan Symbols*. New York: GG Putnam and Sons, 1929.
Gombrich, Ernst H. *Dailė ir iliuzija*. Vertė Rasa Antanavičiūtė. Vilnius: Alma Littera, 2000.
Grabar, Oleg. "Architecture and Art." In *The Genius of Arab Civilization: Source of Renaissance*, edited by John R. Hayes, 77–117. Cambridge: MIT Press, 1975.
Guthrie, William Keith Chambers. *Orpheus and Greek Religion: a Study of the Orphic Movement*. London: Methuen, 1935.
Haase, Rudolf. "Harmonics in Architecture," *Abacus* 2 (1980) 93–113.
Hall, Manley P. *Enciklopediceskoje izlozenije masonskoi, germeticeskoi, kabaliceskoi I rozenkreicerovskoi filosofii*. Novosibirsk: VO Nauka, 1992.
Harvey, John Hooper. *The Medieval Architect*. New York: St. Martin's Press, 1972.
Heller, Sarah Grace. "Light as Glamour: the Luminescent Ideal of Beauty in the Roman de la Rose." *Speculum* 76:4 (2001) 934–59.
Hersey, George L. *Architecture and Geometry in the Age of Baroque*. Chicago: The University of Chicago Press, 2000.
Hitchcock, Henry Russell. *In the Nature of Materials, 1887-1941; the buildings of Frank Lloyd Wright*. New York: Da Capo Press, 1973.
Hügel von, Friedrich. *The Mystical Element of Religion as Studied in Saint Catherine of Genoa and Her Friends*. Vol. I. London: J. M. Dent and Sons, 1923.
Hugh of Saint-Victor. *The Didascalicon: A Medieval Guide to Arts*. Translated by Jerome Taylor. New York: Columbia University Press, 1961.
———. *On the Sacraments of Christian Faith/De Sacramentis*. Translated by R. Deferrari. Cambridge: The Medieval Academy of America, 1951.
Huizinga, Johann. *Viduramžių ruduo*. Vertė Antanas Gailius. Vilnius: Amžius, 1996.
Iamblichus. "The Life of Pythagoras and on the Pythagorean Life" In *The Pythagorean Sourcebook and Library*. Compiled and translated by K. S. Guthrie, et.al. Grand Rapids: Phanes Press, 1987.
Illich, Ivan. *In the Mirror of the Past: Lectures and Addresses 1978-1992*. London: Maryon Boars, 1991.
Johnson, James Rosser. *The Radiance of Chartres: Studies in the Early Stained Glass of the Cathedral*. New York: Random House, 1965.

Kahn, Louis. "Architecture: Silence and Light." In *On the Future of Art*, edited by E. E. Fry, 21–35. New York: The Viking Press, 1970.
Kandinsky, Wassily. *O dukhovnom v iskusstve*. Moskva: Arkhimed, 1992.
Kemp, Martin. "In Praise of Model making; from Leonardo to Beuys." In *Demarco: On the Road to Meikle Segie*, 14–18. London: Kingston University, 2000.
———. *The Science of Art: Optical Themes in Western Art From Brunelleschi to Seurat*. New Haven and London: Yale University Press, 1990.
Képes, György. *The Language of Vision*. New York: Dover Publications, 1995.
Kepler, Johannes. *The Harmony of the World*. Translated by E. A. Aiton et.al. Philadelphia: The American Philosophical Society, 1997
Kostof, Spiro. "The Architect in the Middle Ages." In *The Architect: Chapters into the History of Profession*, 59–95. New York: Oxford University Press, 1990.
Krupp, Edwin C. *Echoes of the Ancient Skies: The Astronomy of Lost Civilizations*. New York: Harper and Row, 1983.
Ladner, Gerhart. *God, Cosmos, and Humankind: The World of Early Christian Symbolism*. Translated by Thomas Dunlap. Berkeley: University of California Press, 1995.
Lancaster, Clay. "Metaphysical Beliefs and Architectural Principles." *The Journal of Aesthetics and Art Criticism* 14:3 (1956) 287–303.
Le Corbusier. *The City of To-morrow and Its Planning*. Translated by Frederick Etchells. London: The Architectural Press, 1947.
Leger, Fernand. "On Monumentality and Color" in Sigfried Giedion. *Architecture, You and Me*, 34–45. Cambridge: Harvard University Press, 1958.
Leonardo da Vinci. *On Painting*, edited and translated by Martin Kemp and Margaret Walker. New Haven and London: Yale University Press, 1989.
Lethaby, William. *Architecture: An Introduction to the History and Theory of the Art of Building*. London: Thornton Butterworth, 1925.
Linton, Harold. *Color in Architecture: Design Methods for Buildings, Interiors, and Urban Spaces*. New York: McGraw-Hill, 1999.
Macrobius. *The Saturnalia*. Translated by Percival Vaughan Davies. Records of civilization: sources and studies: 79. New York: Columbia University Press, 1969.
Mahnke, Frank and Rudolf. *Color and Light in Man-made Environments*. New York: Van Nostrand Reinhold, 1987.
Martin, Rupert John. *Baroque*. New York: Harper and Row, 1977.
Masson, Georgina. *Italian Gardens*. London: Thames and Hudson, 1966.
McDonald, William L. and John A. Pinto. *Hadrian's Villa and Its Legacy*. New Haven: Yale University Press, 1995.
Merkur, Daniel. *Gnosis: An Esoteric Tradition of Mystical Visions and Unions*. Albany: State University of New York Press, 1993.
Milburn, Robert. *Early Christian Art and Architecture*. Berkeley and Los Angeles: University of California Press, 1988.
Mumford, Lewis. *The City in History: Its Origins, its Transformations, and its Prospects*. Harmondsworth: Penguin, 1961.
———. *Technics and Civilization*. New York: Harcourt, Brace and World, 1963.
Nilsson, Jan Olof. "The Need to Harden the Body." In *Nordic Landscapes: The Cultural Studies of Place*, edited by Anders Linde-Laursen and Jan Olof Nilsson, 95–115. NORD, Oslo: Nordic Council of Ministers, 1995.
O'Donoghue, C. *Light and Sound: A Modern Course in Physics*. Dublin: Fallons, 1971.
Ovsianikov, Mikhail. *Istorija estetiki*. Moskva: Iskusstvo, 1964.

Palladio, Andrea. *The Four Books on Architecture*. Introduction by Adolf K. Placzek. New York: Dover Publications, 1965.

———. *Chetyre knigi ob arkhitekture v dvyx tomach*. Tom I. Perevode I. V. Zholtovskiĭ. Moskva: Izdatelsto Csesojuznoj Akademii Arkhitektury, 1936.

Panofsky, Erwin. *Meaning in the Visual Arts*. Harmondsworth: Penguin, 1970.

———. *Studies in Iconology: Humanistic Themes in the Art of the Renaissance*. New York: Harper and Row, 1972.

Paredi, Angelo. *Saint Ambrose: His Life and Times*. Translated by M. J. Costelloe. Indiana: University of Notre Dame Press, 1964.

Pastoureau, Michel. *Blue: The History of a Color*. Princeton: Princeton University Press, 2001.

Pico de Mirandola, Giovanni. "On the Dignity of Man." In *The Renaissance Philosophy of Man*, edited by Ernst Cassirer, et.al. Chicago: University of Chicago Press, 1954.

Plato. *The Republic*. Translated by Francis MacDonald Cornford. London, Oxford and New York: Oxford University Press, 1945.

———. *Timaeus and Critias*. Translated by Desmond Lee. London: Penguin, 1977.

———. "From Philebus." In *Philosophies of Beauty from Socrates to Robert Bridges, Being the Source of Aesthetic Theory*, edited by E. F. Carritt, 29–30. Oxford: Clarendon Press, 1931.

Plommer, Hugh. *Vitruvius and Later Roman Building Manuals*. Cambridge: Cambridge University Press, 1973.

Plotinus. *The Six Enneads*. Great Books of the Western World 17. Translated by Stephen MacKenna and B. S. Page. Chicago and London: Encyclopedia Britannica, 1952.

Porter, Tom. *Architectural Color*. New York: Watson-Guptill Publications, 1982.

Portoghesi, Paolo. *Borromini*. London: Thames and Hudson, 1968.

Rasmussen, Steen Eiler. *Experiencing Architecture*. Cambridge: MIT Press, 1995.

Read, Herbert. *A Concise History of Modern Painting*. New York: Praeger, 1968.

———. *The Meaning of Art*. Harmondsworth: Penguin, 1967.

Richmond, I. A. *Roman Britain*. Harmondsworth: Penguin, 1977.

Riley, Charles A. *Color Codes: Modern Theories of Color in Philosophy, Painting, Architecture, Literature, Music and Psychology*. Hanover: University Press of New England, 1995.

Rogers, Richard. *Cities for a Small Planet*, edited by Philip Gmuchdjian. London: Faber and Faber, 1997.

Roob, Alexander. *Alchemy and Mysticism*. Koln: Taschen, 1997.

Rudofsky, Bernard. *Architecture Without Architects*. New York: Doubleday, 1964.

Ruskin, John. *The Lamp of Beauty: Writings on Art*, edited by Joan Evans. New York: Cornell University Press, 1959.

———. *Lectures on Art: Delivered Before the University of Oxford in Hilary term, 1870*. London: George Allen, 1890.

———. *The Stones of Venice*. London: Allen Unwin, 1898.

Saarinen, Eliel. *The City: Its Growth, Its Decay, Its Future*. New York: Reinhold Publishing Corporation, 1958.

Sabine, Wallace Clement. *Collected Papers on Acoustics*. New York: Dover Publications, 1964.

Santayana, George. In *Philosophies of Beauty from Socrates to Robert Bridges, Being the Source of Aesthetic Theory*, selected and edited by E. F. Carrit, 198–203. Oxford: Clarendon Press, 1931.

Schopenhauer, Arthur. *Pasaulis kaip valia ir vaizdinys*. Vertė Arvydas Šliogeris. Vilnius: Pradai, 1995.
Schreiter, Johann. "The Raw Material Glass as a Light Filter." In *Architectural Stained Glass*, edited by Brian Clarke. New York: Architectural Record Books, 1979, 33
Scott, Geoffrey. *The Architecture of Humanism: A Study in the History of Taste*. New York: Doubleday and Company, 1954.
Scruton, Roger. *The Aesthetics of Architecture*. New York: Princeton University Press, 1980.
Scully, Vincent Joseph. *Architecture: The Natural and the Manmade*. New York: St. Martin's Press, 1991.
———. *Louis I. Kahn*. New York: George Braziller, 1962.
Semper, Gottfried. *The Four Elements of Architecture and Other Writings*. Translated by Henry Francis Malgrave and Wolfgang Herrmann. Cambridge: Cambridge University Press, 1989.
Seznec, Jean. *The Survival of Pagan Gods*. New York: Harper, 1961.
Simonds, John Ormsbee. *Landscape Architecture: A Manual of Site Planning and Design*. New York: McGraw-Hill, 1996.
Simson, Otto Georg von. *The Gothic Cathedral: Origins of Gothic Architecture and the Medieval Concept of Order*. Bollingen 48. New York: Pantheon, 1956.
Sorabji, Richard. "Aristotle on Demarcating Five Senses." In *Articles on Aristotle*. Vol. IV, edited by Jonathan Barnes, et al. London: Duckworth, 1979.
Stokes, Adrian. *The Image in Form. Selected Writings of Adrian Stokes*, edited by Richard Wolheim. New York: Harper and Row, 1972.
Stounberg, Per. "The Overexposed City." In *Nordic Landscapes: Cultural Studies of Place*, edited by Anders Linde-Laursen and Jan Olof Nilsson, 28–45. Oslo: Nord, 1995.
Suger. *Abbot Suger On the Abbey Church of St. Denis and Its Treasures*, edited, translated and annotated by Erwin Panofsky. Princeton: Princeton University Press, 1979.
Taine, Hippolyte. *Meno filosofija*. T. 1. Vertė K. Masiliūnas. Kaunas, 1938.
Taylor, Henry Osborn. *The Medieval Mind: A History of the Development of Thought and Emotion in the Middle Ages*. Vol. II. Cambridge: Harvard University Press, 1951.
Tomlinson, Gary. *Metaphysical Song: An Essay on Opera*. Princeton: Princeton University Press, 1996.
Triggs, Harry Inigo. *Garden Craft in Europe*. London: B. T. Batsford, 1913.
Turner, Fredrick. *Beauty: The Value of Values*. Charlottesville: University Press of Virginia, 1991.
Viollet-le-Duc, Eugene-Emmanuel. *Lectures on Architecture*. Vol. I. Translated by B. Bucknall. New York: Dover Publications, 1987.
Vitruvius. *The Ten Books on Architecture*. Translated by Morris Hicky Morgan. New York: Dover Publications, 1960.
Vorobjovas, Mikalojus. *Vilniaus menas*. Kaunas: Spaudos fondas, 1940.
Wengel, Tassilo. *The Art of Gardening Through the Ages*. Leipzig: Edition Leipzig, 1987.
Wharton, Edith. *Italian Villas and Their Gardens*. New York: Da Capo, 1976.
Whittick, Arnold. *Symbols: Signs and Their Meaning and Uses in Design*. Newton, MA: Charles T. Branford, 1971.
Williamson, Samuel J. and Herman Z. Cummins. *Light and Color in Nature and Art*. New York: John Wiley and Sons, 1983.
Wittkower, Rudolf. *Architectural Principles in the Age of Humanism*. London: Academy Editions, 1973.

Wohl, Hellmut. *The Aesthetics of Italian Renaissance Art: A Reconsideration of Style.* Cambridge: Cambridge University Press, 1999.
Wright, Frank Lloyd. *The Future of Architecture.* New York: Penguin, 1970.
———. *On Architecture.* New York: Duell, Sloan and Pearce, 1941.
———. *Writings and Buildings.* Selected by Edgar Kaufmann and Ben Raeburn. New York: Penguin, 1960.

www.ingramcontent.com/pod-product-compliance
Lightning Source LLC
Chambersburg PA
CBHW071332190426
43193CB00041B/1568